# CONTENTS

# INTRODUCTION

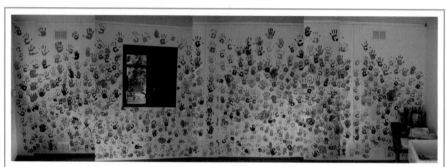

Hands, courtesy of Old Ford School, Room 13.

This book is about the many ways in which people are creating new and more effective answers to the biggest challenges of our times: how to cut our carbon footprint; how to keep people healthy; and how to end poverty.

It describes the methods and tools for innovation being used across the world and across different sectors – the public and private sectors, civil society and the household – in the overlapping fields of the social economy, social entrepreneurship and social enterprise. It draws on inputs from hundreds of organisations to document the many methods currently being used around the world.

The materials we've gathered here are intended to support all those involved in social innovation: policymakers who can help to create the right conditions; foundations and philanthropists who can fund and support; social organisations trying to meet social needs more effectively; and social entrepreneurs and innovators themselves.

In other fields, methods for innovation are well understood. In medicine, science, and to a lesser degree in business, there are widely accepted ideas, tools and approaches. There are strong institutions and many people whose job requires them to be good at taking ideas from inception to impact. There is little comparable in the social field, despite the richness and vitality of social innovation. Most people trying to innovate are aware of only a fraction of the methods they could be using.

This book, and the series of which it is a part, attempt to fill this gap. In this volume, we map out the hundreds of methods for social innovation as a first step to developing a knowledge base. In the other volume of the Social Innovator series, we look at specific methods in greater depth, exploring ways of developing workable ideas and setting up a social venture in a way that ensures its financial sustainability; and that its structures of accountability, governance and ownership resonate with its social mission.[1] We have also launched an accompanying website, www.socialinnovator.info, to gather comments, case studies and new methods.

We're also very conscious of what's not in here. This is very much a first cut: there are many methods we haven't covered; many parts of the world that aren't well represented (including Africa and the Middle East); and many which we've only been able to describe in a very summary form.

The field we cover is broad. Social innovation doesn't have fixed boundaries: it happens in all sectors, public, non-profit and private. Indeed, much of the most creative action is happening at the boundaries between sectors, in fields as diverse as fair trade, distance learning, hospices, urban farming, waste reduction and restorative justice.

Nevertheless, definitions have their place. Our interest is in innovations that are social both in their ends and in their means. Specifically, we define social innovations as new ideas (products, services and models) that simultaneously meet social needs and create new social relationships or collaborations. In other words, they are innovations that are both good for society *and* enhance society's capacity to act.[2]

## The context for social innovation

Why has social innovation moved centre stage over the last decade? The main reason is that existing structures and policies have found it impossible to crack some of the most pressing issues of our times – such as climate change, the worldwide epidemic of chronic disease, and widening inequality.

### Intractable social problems
The classic tools of government policy on the one hand, and market solutions on the other, have proved grossly inadequate. The market, by itself, lacks the incentives and appropriate models to solve many of these issues. Where there are market failures (due to non-competitive markets, externalities or public

goods), these tasks have fallen either to the state or civil society. However, current policies and structures of government have tended to reinforce old rather than new models. The silos of government departments are poorly suited to tackling complex problems which cut across sectors and nation states. Civil society lacks the capital, skills and resources to take promising ideas to scale.

### Rising costs

The prospective cost of dealing with these issues threatens to swamp public budgets, and in the case of climate change, or healthcare in the US, private budgets as well. To take only one instance, if radical policies cannot stem the increase in chronic diseases, the cost of healthcare is forecast to rise from 9 per cent to 12.5 per cent of GDP in the UK in 15 years and, according to the US Congressional Budget Office, from 16 per cent of GDP in 2007 to 25 per cent in 2025, rising to 37 per cent in 2050. As in climate change, pollution control, waste reduction, poverty and welfare programmes, and other fields such as criminal justice or traffic congestion, the most effective policies are preventative. But effective prevention has been notoriously difficult to introduce, in spite of its apparent economic and social benefits.

### Old paradigms

As during earlier technological and social transformations, there is a disjunction between existing structures and institutions and what's needed now. This is as true for the private as for the social economy. New paradigms tend to flourish in areas where the institutions are most open to them, and where the forces of the old are weak. So, for example, there is more innovation around self-management of diseases and public health than around hospitals; more innovation around recycling and energy efficiency than around large scale energy production; more innovation around public participation than in parliaments and assemblies; and more innovation around active ageing than around pension provision.

## An emerging social economy

Much of this innovation is pointing towards a new kind of economy. It combines some old elements and many new ones. We describe it as a 'social economy' because it melds features which are very different from economies based on the production and consumption of commodities. Its key features include:

- The intensive use of distributed networks to sustain and manage relationships, helped by broadband, mobile and other means of communication.

- Blurred boundaries between production and consumption.

- An emphasis on collaboration and on repeated interactions, care and maintenance rather than one-off consumption.

- A strong role for values and missions.

Two themes – sometimes clashing, sometimes coinciding – give it its distinctive character. One comes from technology: the spread of networks; creation of global infrastructures for information; and social networking tools. The other comes from culture and values: the growing emphasis on the human dimension; on putting people first; giving democratic voice; and starting with the individual and relationships rather than systems and structures.

Much of this economy is formed around distributed systems, rather than centralised structures. It handles complexity not by standardisation and simplification imposed from the centre, but by distributing complexity to the margins – to the local managers and workers on the shop floor, as well as to the consumers themselves.

As a result, the role of the consumer changes from a passive to an active player: to a producer in their own right. Retail purchases that have been cast as the end point of the linear process of mass production are redefined as part of a circular process of household production and reproduction. The so-called consumer doubles as a domestic producer – a cook, a mother, a carer, a shopper, a driver, a nurse, a gardener, a teacher or student – entailing so much of what makes us human. This domestic sphere has previously been seen as outside the economy, as too complex and ungovernable, but has now come to be recognised as economically critical, with all the needs for support, tools, skills and advice that being a producer entails.

In both the market and state economies, the rise of distributed networks has coincided with a marked turn towards the human, the personal and the individual. This has brought a greater interest in the quality of relationships (what Jim Maxmin and Shoshana Zuboff call the 'support economy'); it has led to lively innovation around personalisation (from new types of mentor to personal accounts); a new world rich in information and feedback (such as AMEE, tracking carbon outputs in 150 different countries); growing interest in pathways (for example from early childhood into adulthood) and service journeys (whether of a patient through a health system or a passenger through an airport).

With this emphasis on the individual has come an interest in their experience as well as in formal outcomes, in subjective feedback as well as the quantitative metrics of the late 20th century state and economy (hence the rise of innovations like the Expert Patients programmes, or Patient Opinion). Public policy has also turned towards the household, through innovations like nurse-family partnerships and green concierges.

## What is distinct about social innovation?

What is it about social innovation which is distinct from innovation in different fields? The definition we provided above emphasises that social innovation is distinctive both in its outcomes and in its relationships, in the new forms of cooperation and collaboration that it brings. As a result, the processes, metrics, models and methods used in innovation in the commercial or technological fields, for example, are not always directly transferable to the social economy.

### Measuring success
Measuring success in the social economy is particularly problematic. In the market the simple and generally unambiguous measures are scale, market share and profit. In the social field the very measures of success may be contested as well as the tools for achieving results. Is it good or bad to cut car use? Is it good or bad to replace professional care by voluntary care? Is a good school one that excels at exam results? Is it always a good thing for an NGO to grow bigger? The answers are never straightforward and are themselves the subject of argument, evaluation and assessment. As we show, there has been a great deal of innovation around metrics – from tools to judge the impact of a particular project or programme to meta-analyses and assessments of much larger processes of social change.

### Organisational forms
And then there are the organisational forms for innovation itself. We show that many innovations take shape within organisations – public agencies, social enterprises, mutuals, co-ops, charities, companies as well as loose associations. But the many examples set out below also show a field that is grappling with how to escape the constraints of organisation so as to make innovation itself open and social: posting ideas and welcoming responses from

anyone; involving users at every stage as well as experts, bureaucrats and professionals; designing platforms which make it easy to assemble project teams or virtual organisations.

Organisational forms are important for any kind of innovation, but particularly for the ones that are truly systemic in nature. As we show these invariably involve more than a new service or model: they also create a change in relationships of power, and a change in how people think and see. Invariably, systems changes stretch far beyond the boundaries of any single organisation.

**Coalitions and networks**
Coalitions and networks are increasingly turning out to be the key to successful change (this is well described in Stephen Goldsmith's forthcoming book on civic entrepreneurship in the USA). Whereas in business the firm is the key agent of innovation, in the social field the drive is more likely to come from a wider network, perhaps linking some commissioners in the public sector, providers in social enterprises, advocates in social movements, and entrepreneurs in business. This is one of many reasons why it's misleading to translate business models directly into the social field. For example, trying too hard to privatise ideas, or protect their IP, is more likely to stall the innovation process than to galvanise it. But public structures can be equally inhibiting if they try to squeeze a new idea into the logic of siloed departments or professions.

No one knows what will emerge from the feverish experiment, trial and error and rapid learning that are accompanying the birth of this new economy. But we can be certain that its emergence will encourage ever more interest in how innovation can best be supported, orchestrated and harnessed to speed up the invention and adoption of better solutions.

## Methods

Innovation isn't just a matter of luck, eureka moments or alchemy. Nor is it exclusively the province of brilliant individuals. Innovation can be managed, supported and nurtured. And anyone, if they want, can become part of it.

These are some of the key messages that we've taken from the most creative thinkers about innovation – such as John Kao and Rosabeth Moss Kanter, Mark Moore, Manuel Castells and Roberto Unger. They have shown that social innovation is a relatively open field and a relatively open process. Certainly, some are more equal than others – and governments with large budgets and law-making powers can achieve large-scale change more easily than small community groups. Yet most social change is neither purely top-down nor bottom-up. It involves alliances between the top and the bottom, or between what we call the 'bees' (the creative individuals with ideas and energy) and the 'trees' (the big institutions with the power and money to make things happen to scale).

In what follows we describe many hundreds of methods being used for innovation around the world. They range from ways of thinking to very practical tools for finance or design. Some of them are specific to sectors – government, business or charity. Some are specific to national cultures. But there are many common patterns, and one of the purposes of this project has been to encourage cross-pollination.

Much innovation comes from the creative blending of ideas from multiple sources. For example, bringing together diagnostic computer programmes, call centres and nurses to provide new kinds of healthcare; bringing together the very old idea of 'circles of support' brought within the criminal justice system; or bringing the idea of enforceable rights into the world of the family and childhood.

The tools of innovation will also develop through creative blending and recombination of disparate elements and ideas. We're already seeing, for example, innovators combining the funding methods used for science and venture capital with those from tendering and grant giving. Others are combining ethnography, visualisation techniques from product design, user-involvement ideas from social movements, and commissioning methods from the public sector. Business has already adopted some of the models for mobilising networks of users that were developed by the third sector in the 1960s and 1970s. Conversely, some NGOs are learning from venture capital not only how to finance emerging ideas, but also how to kill off ones that aren't advancing fast enough to free up resources. Our hope is that by gathering many methods together we will accelerate these processes of creative recombination and experimentation.

**The structure of the book**
To structure the many methods we've collected we look at them through three different lenses:

In Part 1 of this book, we look at **the processes of innovation**. We describe the stages of innovation as spreading outwards from prompts and ideas to scale and growth. Some innovations do develop in this linear way, and we find this framework useful for thinking more rigorously about methods. But many do not develop in a purely linear fashion: some go quickly to scale and then have to adapt fast in the light of experience; often, the end use of an innovation will be very different from the one that was originally envisaged; sometimes action precedes understanding and sometimes taking action crystallises the idea. And always there is an iterative circling back as new insights change the nature of the innovation. Nevertheless, these processes do indicate a trend in the development of an innovation and we hope that the spiral model can provide a common language for thinking about how to support innovation more systematically.

In Part 2, we look at the **key institutions** which help to make innovation happen: funds, agencies, brokers, incubators, and intermediaries. In the social field these institutions remain much less developed than in other fields. But they are multiplying rapidly, and bringing new lessons in how best to link ideas with their best applications.

In Part 3, we look at **the enabling conditions for innovation**, including those within each economy: the public sector, the grant economy of civil society, the private sector, and the household. Some of these conditions are about structures and laws, others are about cultures.

This book is a work in progress. It is very much a snapshot, designed to encourage further contributions. The methods for social innovation should be a common property, and should evolve through shared learning. Social innovations often struggle against the odds – all of our chances of success will increase if we can share our experiences and quickly reflect on what works and what doesn't.

## End notes

1. Murray, R., Caulier-Grice, J. and Mulgan, G. (2009) 'Social Venturing.' The Social Innovator Series. London: NESTA.

2. In their article for the Stanford Social Innovation Review, Phills, Deiglmeier and Miller define social innovation as: "a novel solution to a social problem that is more effective, efficient, sustainable, or just than existing solutions and for which the value created accrues primarily to society as a whole rather than private individuals. A social innovation can be a product, production process, or technology (much like innovation in general), but it can also be a principle, an idea, a piece of legislation, a social movement, an intervention, or some combination of them." NESTA defines social innovation as: "innovation that is explicitly for the social and public good. It is innovation inspired by the desire to meet social needs which can be neglected by traditional forms of private market provision and which have often been poorly served or unresolved by services organised by the state. Social innovation can take place inside or outside of public services. It can be developed by the public, private or third sectors, or users and communities – but equally, some innovation developed by these sectors does not qualify as social innovation because it does not directly address major social challenges." The OECD's LEED Programme (Local Economic and Employment Development), which includes a Forum on Social Innovations, has developed its own definition. The Forum defines social innovation as that which concerns: "conceptual, process or product change, organisational change and changes in financing, and can deal with new relationships with stakeholders and territories. 'Social innovation' seeks new answers to social problems by: identifying and delivering new services that improve the quality of life of individuals and communities; identifying and implementing new labour market integration processes, new competencies, new jobs, and new forms of participation, as diverse elements that each contribute to improving the position of individuals in the workforce."

# SECTION 1: THE PROCESS OF SOCIAL INNOVATION

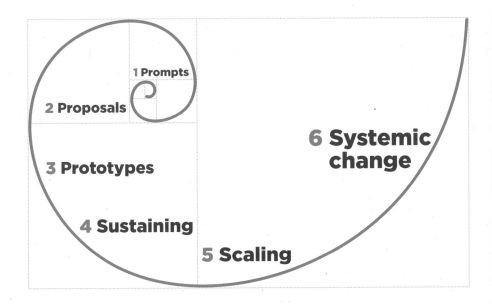

1 Prompts

2 Proposals

3 Prototypes

4 Sustaining

5 Scaling

6 Systemic change

## The six stages of social innovation

We have identified six stages that take ideas from inception to impact. These stages are not always sequential (some innovations jump straight into 'practice' or even 'scaling'), and there are feedback loops between them. They can also be thought of as overlapping spaces, with distinct cultures and skills. They provide a useful framework for thinking about the different kinds of support that innovators and innovations need in order to grow.

1)  **Prompts, inspirations and diagnoses.** In this stage we include all the factors which highlight the need for innovation – such as crisis, public spending cuts, poor performance, strategy – as well as the inspirations which spark it, from creative imagination to new evidence. This stage involves diagnosing the problem and framing the question in such a way that the root causes of the problem, not just its symptoms, will be tackled. Framing the right question is halfway to finding the right solution. This means going beyond symptoms to identifying the causes of a particular problem.

2)  **Proposals and ideas.** This is the stage of idea generation. This can involve formal methods – such as design or creativity methods to widen the menu of options available. Many of the methods help to draw in insights and experiences from a wide range of sources.

3)  **Prototyping and pilots.** This is where ideas get tested in practice. This can be done through simply trying things out, or through more formal pilots, prototypes and randomised controlled trials. The process of refining and testing ideas is particularly important in the social economy because it's through iteration, and trial and error, that coalitions gather strength (for example, linking users to professionals) and conflicts are resolved (including battles with entrenched interests). It's also through these processes that measures of success come to be agreed upon.

4)  **Sustaining.** This is when the idea becomes everyday practice. It involves sharpening ideas (and often streamlining them), and identifying income streams to ensure the long term financial sustainability of the firm, social enterprise or charity, that will carry the innovation forward. In the public sector this means identifying budgets, teams and other resources such as legislation.

5)  **Scaling and diffusion.** At this stage there are a range of strategies
    for growing and spreading an innovation – from organisational growth,
    through licensing and franchising to federations and looser diffusion.
    Emulation and inspiration also play a critical role in spreading an idea or
    practice. Demand matters as much as supply: how market demand, or
    demand from commissioners and policymakers is mobilised to spread a
    successful new model. This process is often referred to as 'scaling', and
    in some cases the word is appropriate, as the innovation is generalised
    within an organisation or the organisation itself expands. But scaling is
    a concept from the mass production age, and innovations take hold in
    the social economy in many other ways, whether through inspiration and
    emulation, or through the provision of support and know-how from one
    to another in a more organic and adaptive kind of growth.

6)  **Systemic change.** This is the ultimate goal of social innovation.
    Systemic change usually involves the interaction of many elements:
    social movements, business models, laws and regulations, data and
    infrastructures, and entirely new ways of thinking and doing. Systemic
    change generally involves new frameworks or architectures made up of
    many smaller innovations. Social innovations commonly come up against
    the barriers and hostility of an old order. Pioneers may sidestep these
    barriers, but the extent to which they can grow will often depend on the
    creation of new conditions to make the innovations economically viable.
    These conditions include new technologies, supply chains, institutional
    forms, skills, and regulatory and fiscal frameworks. Systemic innovation
    commonly involves changes in the public sector, private sector, grant
    economy and household sector, usually over long periods of time.

In this part of the book we explore each of these stages in depth, with a
section listing some of the main methods used for each one.

# 1 PROMPTS, INSPIRATIONS AND DIAGNOSES

## Framing the question

All innovations start with a central idea. But the idea itself is often prompted by an experience or event or new evidence which brings to light a social need or injustice. Some organisations initiate the prompts themselves – using feedback systems to identify possible problems. Creative leaders can use symbols and demonstrations to prompt social imagination. In many cases, research, mapping and data collection are used to uncover problems, as a first step to identifying solutions.

One of the critical challenges at this stage is in identifying the right problem. A 'good' problem contains within it the seeds of the solution. The trick is in framing the question. Like medicine, the key issue in social policy is one of diagnosis, of going beyond the symptom to the cause. As Curitiba's Jaime Lerner explains, a problem of parking is merely a reflection of a problem in the public transport system. In such a case seeking solutions to the wrong problem can often make them worse. In other cases, it is a matter of breaking down a general problem into manageable bits, of getting down to the actionable parts.

The prompts are triggers for action. They may take the form of imperatives, in that some action is needed without specifying what that action is, for example a budget crisis or a natural disaster. Such prompts are closely linked to problem recognition, and the myriad ways in which a problem comes to light and commands attention. Once the problem is recognised, it needs to be interrogated, and contextualised. This is the process of reformulating the problem in such a way as to stimulate workable solutions. Those running ideas competitions for the crowdsourcing of innovations say that it is the stage of framing a good question which is the key to the competition's success.[1]

All of the methods that follow are not only prompts, but also steps towards refining the question and generating a solution.

## Triggers and inspirations

Here we describe some of the triggers and inspirations that prompt innovation, that demand action on an issue, or that mobilise belief that action is possible.

1)  **Crisis.** Necessity is often the mother of invention, but crises can also crush creativity. One of the definitions of leadership is the ability to use the smallest crisis to achieve the greatest positive change. Many nations have used economic and social crises to accelerate reform and innovation and in some cases have used the crisis to deliberately accelerate social innovation. New Orleans after Hurricane Katrina is one example (LousianaRebuilds.info or the New Orleans Institute for Resilience and Innovation); China's much more effective response to the Szechuan earthquake is another. Both, in very different ways, institutionalised innovation as part of the response.

2)  **Efficiency savings.** The need to cut public expenditure often requires services to be designed and delivered in new ways. Major cuts can rarely be achieved through traditional efficiency measures. Instead they require systems change – for example, to reduce numbers going into prison, or to reduce unnecessary pressures on hospitals. The right kinds of systems thinking can open up new possibilities.[2]

3)  **Poor performance** highlights the need for change within services. This can act as a spur for finding new ways of designing and delivering public services. The priority will usually be to adopt innovations from elsewhere.[3]

4)  **New technologies** can be adapted to meet social needs better or deliver services more effectively. Examples include computers in classrooms, the use of assistive devices for the elderly, or implants to cut teenage pregnancy. Through experiment it is then discovered how these work best (such as the discovery that giving computers to two children to share is more effective for education than giving them one each). Any new technology becomes a prompt. Artificial intelligence, for example,

Climate Camp protestors at Heathrow Airport. Image courtesy of Gary Austin – Radical Images.

has been used in family law in Australia and to help with divorce negotiations in the US.

5)   **New evidence** brings to light new needs and new solutions for dealing with these needs, such as lessons from neuroscience being applied to childcare and early years' interventions or knowledge about the effects of climate change.

6)   **Urban acupuncture.** Symbolic moves can give energy to an area, and create a context for social innovation. Jaime Lerner, the former Mayor of Curitiba (Brazil), coined the phrase 'urban acupuncture' to describe the effect that some small-scale symbolic projects can have in creating points of energy that make a city more open to innovation.[4] An example that incorporates a number of these elements is the Cheonggyecheon project in Seoul. Mayor Lee Myung-bak removed a two-tier motorway to reclaim the old river, which meandered across the city centre. The project, which entailed an intensive process of planning, consultation and construction, won the prize for architecture at the Venice Biennale of

2005. It symbolised a greener, more human phase of development for the city, as well as reinforcing Seoul's role as a centre for creative industries, including software, gaming and music. Other landmark projects that gave people a licence to be creative in other fields include: Angel of the North in Gateshead, the fourth plinth in Trafalgar Square, Tirana's move to repaint houses in vivid colours, and the Waterfire in Rhode Island.

## Recognising problems

Problems need to be recognised. Too often they are hidden, or marginalised. Or there is a belief that nothing can be done about them. Much research is about bringing problems to light. A lot of politics is about getting problems a hearing.

### Research and mapping

Many innovations are triggered by new data and research. In recent years, there has been a rise in the use of mapping techniques to reveal hidden needs and unused assets. The Latin origin of the word evidence (evidentia) is to make clear and visible, and visibility generates ideas.

7) **Mapping needs** to estimate the existence, nature and distribution of the actual and potential need for goods and services, specifically where the need is a social need. There are multiple approaches, including: epidemiological studies, surveys, the use of social indicators, socio-demographic datasets, and 'Voices of the Poor' projects. The Young Foundation's Mapping Needs Project, and a parallel project in Portugal, have developed a comprehensive set of quantitative and qualitative methods. These aim to understand underlying causes – for example looking at the importance of 'adaptive resilience' in explaining why some individuals, families and communities cope well with shocks while others do not.[5]

8) **Identifying differential needs and capacities** through market research, consumer categories and geo-demographic segmentation techniques. Segmentation is becoming increasingly important to social innovation in fields such as health (sometimes under the misleading label 'social marketing') – where policies and programmes that work well for one group may fail for others. Where governments in the past focused on typical or 'average' citizens, today policy and provision is much more interested in disaggregating data. There are also a range of tools for combining and mining data to reveal new needs and patterns.

These sites show how to run competitions for 'mash up' ideas from citizens using government data, such as Sunlight Labs and Show Us a Better Way.

9) **Mapping physical assets.** Within the social economy, especially amongst artists, entrepreneurs and community groups, there is a long tradition of taking advantage of empty, abandoned or derelict buildings and spaces. Mapping exercises can be employed to take stock of the local area, identifying empty spaces and opportunities for re-use. In Croatia, for example, Platforma 9.18 mapped out what remained of the built landscape of Zagreb after the Yugoslav civil wars of the 1990s. They mapped an extensive diagram of abandoned factories, offices and scraps of land, which they suggested could be used for cultural events. In the UK, the website Report Empty Homes, sponsored by the Empty Homes Agency, allows citizens to report empty properties around the UK.

10) **Mapping systems** such as participative mapping and sectoral analysis, as practised for example in the Kerala People's Planning Campaign.

11) **Mapping flows** of people, goods and messages often uncovers unseen patterns and possibilities. Some of the influential planning movements in Scandinavia in the 1950s and 1960s emphasised flow as the key to understanding cities. More recently, a focus on flow and service journeys has been central to the continuous improvement ideas of Deming and firms like Toyota.

12) **Communities researching themselves** to identify their own needs and solutions to those needs. This includes participatory methods such as those used in PRA (below). But other examples include user-led and peer research, based on the premise that people are best placed to identify their own needs and express their own ideas or solutions. User-led research has especially developed amongst long term users of health and social care services. Service users are responsible for all stages of the research process – from design, recruitment, ethics and data collection to data analysis, writing up, and dissemination. One example is the independent, user-controlled network, Shaping Our Lives, which started as a research and development project and now works with a wide range of service users across the UK.

Participators mapping with a smallholder in Kerala: a time mapping of the different crops, their use/market, and what kind of fertiliser if any that they used; and a map of the farm (on the table) showing the crops that are currently being grown. The young man sitting at the table is the farmer's son. He is currently studying, and hopes to work in the Middle East, but intends to return to the farm to take over when his father retires. Image courtesy of Robin Murray.

13) **Participatory Rural Appraisal (PRA)** involves a range of techniques such as interviews, mapping, focus groups and events to understand community views on particular issues. The aim is to engage local people in both the identification of problems and the design and implementation of solutions. This approach has been used by the World Bank, Action Aid, the Aga Khan Foundation, the Ford Foundation and others. PRA uses a range of visualisation techniques – such as mapping as a tool for learning about sexual health and reproduction, and physical mapping to represent the local area. These maps illustrate the boundary of a particular village or settlement and the social and economic infrastructure – roads, water supply, agricultural land, crops and schools.[6]

14) **Ethnographic research techniques.** Ethnography is a holistic approach to research developed by anthropologists in order to understand people within their social and cultural contexts. The underlying theoretical basis of ethnography is that people's actions and thoughts are dependent on a vast range of factors, and what they say and do in one context is not necessarily what they actually do in another. To fully understand peoples' behaviour, opinions and decision-making processes, a researcher must therefore spend time with them in their various physical and social environments. The primary method of the ethnographer is 'participant observation'. This involves the immersion of the researcher into the lives of those that they are studying. The ethnographer seeks not only to observe and enquire about situations people are faced with, but to participate within them. The exact nature of the participation is balanced with cultural and practical sensitivity, but in various settings it will involve the ethnographer spending a day shadowing a respondent in their home, educational, and social environments.

15) **Action research** is a method designed to encourage reflective and collective problem formulation and problem solving. It seeks to replace the usual relationship of 'researcher' and 'researched' with a more collaborative, iterative relationship where the emphasis is on research 'with' as opposed to 'on' people. Rather than merely detailing an environment in descriptive form, action research is normatively geared toward prescriptions emerging out of the data which can be employed for the improvement of future action.

16) **Literature surveys and reviews** to bring together research evidence and identify promising new approaches, including models that can be borrowed from other fields. An outstanding recent example is New Zealand academic John Hattie's work on schools, 'Visible Learning', which brings together 800 meta-analyses of what works, including many counter-intuitive findings.[7]

## The circuit of information

New needs can also be brought to the fore through effective feedback systems. Such systems can help practitioners and front line staff understand the needs of users and better tailor services accordingly. In industry and commerce the capacity to collect and analyse large quantities of data has been the basis for remarkable changes – for example: in flexible manufacturing, and in the practice of retailing. In Japanese factories data is collected by front line workers, and then discussed in quality circles that include technicians. Statistical production techniques reveal patterns that are not evident to those directly involved, and have been transferred with remarkable results to the medical treatment of patients in the US.[8]

17) **Feedback systems** from front line staff and users to senior managers and staff. Feedback loops are a necessary precondition for learning, reviewing and improving. This could include front line service research to tap into the expertise of practitioners and front line staff, using techniques such as in-depth interviews and ethnographic/observation methods. User feedback on service quality, including web-based models such as Patient Opinion and I Want Great Care that hold service providers to account, or the Kafka Brigades in the Netherlands. Another example is Fix My Street, which allows local residents to report local problems (such as graffiti, broken paving slabs, street lighting and so on) directly to local authorities. And, in the US, a new free application called iBurgh allows residents to snap iPhone photos of local problems, like potholes, graffiti and abandoned cars, and send them to the city's 311 complaint system, embedded with GPS data pinpointing the exact location of the problem. These complaints will then get forwarded to the relevant city department.

18) **Integrated user-centred data** such as Electronic Patient Records in the UK, which, when linked through grid and cloud computing models provide the capacity to spot emerging patterns: A contrasting integrated system for monitoring renal patients has led to dramatic improvements in survival rates and cost reductions in the United States.[9]

19) **Citizen-controlled data**, such as the health records operated by Group Health in Seattle, and the ideas being developed by Mydex that adapt vendor relationship-management software tools to put citizens in control of the personal data held by big firms and public agencies. This allows them to monitor their conditions and chart their own behaviour and actions.

20) **Holistic services** include phone based services such as New York's 311 service which provide a database that can be analysed for patterns of recurring problems and requests.

21) **Tools for handling knowledge across a system**. One example is Intellipedia, the US intelligence community's wiki for sharing

information. It has proved particularly effective for sharing sensitive information across departments. It provides the basis for recognising gaps and overlaps, and indicates the possibilities for service co-ordination and improvement.

## New perspectives

New ideas are often prompted by new ways of seeing that put familiar things in a new light. These may be paradigms or models, and may be encouraged by formal roles that are designed to help organisations think in fresh ways.

22) **Generative paradigms** provide new ways of thinking and doing. Ideas lead to other ideas. Examples include the idea of disability rights, closed-loop manufacturing, zero-carbon housing or lifelong learning. The most fertile paradigms generate many hypotheses, and from these come new ideas and policies.[10]

23) **Generative 'scripts'.** Bart Nooteboom has shown that some of the most important innovation involves the creation and embedding of new patterns of behaviour. An example from the private sector is the rise of fast food retailing which created a new 'script' for having a meal. Where the traditional restaurant script was: choose, be served, eat, then pay, the self service/fast food script is: choose, pay, carry food to table, eat and clear up. New 'scripts' are emerging right across the public sector, in areas like recycling, personalised learning in schools and self-managed healthcare, and are likely to be critical to future productivity gains in public services.[11]

24) **Changing roles.** Innovations may be triggered when professionals and managers change their roles – some doctors spend one day each year in the role of patients, and some local authority chief executives spend time on the reception desk. Prison reform has historically been advanced when members of the elite have undergone spells in prison. Some innovative businesses rotate their directors (and Switzerland has long changed its Prime Minister every year).

25) **Artists in Residence** such as Mierle Laderman Ukeles, a conceptual and performance artist working in what she called 'maintenance art'. She was employed for many years by the New York Sanitation Department as an Artist in Residence. Her first project was called 'Touch Sanitation', and was provoked by what she had found to be the degradation and invisibility of garbage workers.[12] She set out to do the

opposite of what social science does, namely sample, abstract and select. She decided to shake the hands of every one of the 8,500 employees of the Department, across 59 districts, carefully mapped by place and time. To each of them she said "Thank you for keeping New York City alive". MindLab in Denmark has also invited artists to inspire civil servants and provide a new perspective on policy issues. MindLab recently invited artist Olafur Eliasson to take part in an inter-ministerial working group on climate change to develop new policy initiatives for Denmark's forthcoming climate change strategy for businesses (see also method 280 for more information on MindLab).

26) **Thinkers in Residence** such as those in South Australia and Manitoba, where thinkers are employed by governments to stimulate creative thinking and practical innovation. The Thinker in Residence programme in South Australia started in 2003. Each year, up to four internationally renowned experts spend between two and six months helping the government to identify problems and explore original solutions on issues ranging from climate change to childcare.

27) **A-teams** are groups of young public servants commissioned to develop innovative solutions. The model has been used in many places. In South Australia, A-teams have also commissioned young film-makers and artists to work alongside the policy team to create lateral comments on the issues.

**Making problems visible and tangible**
Social phenomena are not automatically visible. One of the crucial roles of social science, and of statistics, is to bring patterns to the surface that are otherwise invisible to people living within them, or governing them. Seeing an issue in a new way can then prompt more creative thinking about alternatives.

28) **Tools for visibility.** Mapping, visualisations, storyboards, photographs and video interviews are all tools used by design agencies – a dynamic field concerned with visualisations of complexity. One example is the Design Council's project with diabetes sufferers in Bolton. During the course of their project, the Design Council found that many people with diabetes often find it difficult to make the lifestyle changes they need to stay healthy. The designers devised new ways of helping those with diabetes talk about these difficulties with doctors. They created a pack of cards, each with their own message. These cards were then used by health professionals to help people to manage their diabetes more effectively.

These are the cards developed by the Design Council as part of their project with diabetes sufferers in Bolton. The cards were used to help patients talk about diabetes and their experiences of living with it in a non-medical way. Image courtesy of The Design Council and Giulio Mazzarini.

29)  **Walking** makes problems visible and at the same time prompts ideas.
In the words of Werner Herzog, 'the world reveals itself to those who
travel on foot'. Techniques include the Situationists' dérive, or more
contemporary methods such as those used by Stalker Lab in Rome,
which has brought to light the situation of the Roma. In India, the Shodh
Yatra, organised by the Honey Bee Network is one of the best examples
of the power of walking. In one week, walkers (farmers, scientists and
researchers) travel hundreds of kilometres across rural India to unearth,
share and disseminate sustainable solutions to local issues including
conservation, organic farming and biodiversity, as well as health and
nutrition. During the day, walkers pass through farming land – usually
accompanied by local farmers and labourers who discuss and reflect
on their farming practices. In the evening, walkers stay in villages and
hold meetings with local residents to discuss activities of the Honey

Walking to discover innovation at the grassroots. The Shodh Yatra, organised
by the Honey Bee Network, is a journey of discovery and exploration. In
one week, walkers (farmers, scientists and researchers) travel hundreds of
kilometres across rural India to unearth, share and disseminate sustainable
solutions to local issues including conservation, organic farming and
biodiversity, as well as health and nutrition. Image courtesy of Alice Smeets.

Bee Network and to share insights and knowledge of innovations from other parts of India. It is an opportunity for the walkers and villagers to share and reflect on innovative practice. There are also prizes – there are biodiversity competitions, recipe competitions and a felicitation ceremony for creative villagers.

30) **Media Spotlight.** The media can provide oxygen to support innovations, or prompt action on social problems. Al Gore's film, 'An Inconvenient Truth' did much to raise awareness about the dangers of climate change. 'Black Gold' on coffee and 'The End of the Line' on fishing are also good examples of linking film-making to social change, with clear actions for individual viewers to take. Other examples of the media as a prompt include programmes that create public pressure and encourage broader media campaigns. Seminal programmes include the 1960s BBC drama 'Cathy Come Home' which raised awareness about homelessness, the 1989 BBC documentary 'John's Not Mad', which followed a young man suffering from Tourette syndrome and did much to expose some of the misperceptions around the disease.

## Commanding attention

In today's media-intensive environment, one of the most valuable resources is attention. Without it, social change is painfully slow. A key stage in many innovations is securing people's attention – particularly of those with power.

31) **Complaints Choirs** gather groups of citizens to discuss complaints and turn them into lyrics that are performed as songs. The idea was first conceived in Finland, first put into practice in Birmingham in England, and has now spread around the world. There are, for example, 11 complaints choirs in Korea.

32) **User and public pressure** can force change. Politics remains the most powerful channel for pressure but feedback can also be organised through many routes, from surveys and websites to user representation on management boards and committees.

33) **Campaigns** which channel dissatisfaction and discontent into a search for innovations. For example, the disability rights movement has prompted innovations in technologies, buildings and public policy. Other examples include Greenpeace's 'Green My Apple' campaign, which prompted Apple to change its policy and stop using a number of hazardous materials, or campaigns on overfishing which prompted

The Kwanak Hanullim Complaints Choir at the Festival of Complaints Choirs organised by the Hope Institute in Seoul, South Korea in 2008. Courtesy of the Hope Institute.

An average European flight produces over 400kg of greenhouse gases per passenger, approximately the weight of an adult polar bear. This is a still from Plane Stupid's new cinema ad against airport expansion and aviation's climate impact, from creative agency Mother, directed by Daniel Kleinman and produced by Rattling Stick. Image courtesy of Plane Stupid.

new methods for using GPS to track ships. Increasingly, direct action is being used as an effective means of raising awareness within the green and environmental movements. Examples of direct action include Plane Stupid, a network of protest groups opposing airport expansion and aviation's climate impact.

## From symptom to cause

Diagnosing problems is a first step to developing solutions. A key challenge is to get to the underlying causes of a problem. To a hammer every problem looks like a nail. It's always easier to deal with symptoms rather than causes. Some of the methods for digging deeper involve the analysis of systems while others involve mobilising people's own experiences and perspectives.

34) **The diagnostic process.** The gathering and presentation of data requires a process of interpretation. This should ideally include those involved in the implementation of ideas and those affected by the proposals. Often there are conflicting interpretations, which can only be settled by trying out the suggested alternatives in practice.

35) **Diagnostic professions.** Many professions – from medicine to engineering – have their own framework for diagnosis, of looking beyond symptoms to causes. Some of the most interesting insights come from analysts of human behaviour – anthropologists, psychoanalysts, and sociologists. In analysing an issue or a set of data, it is useful to have the perspectives of a variety of professional disciplines, as each 'reading' will suggest different ideas for action.

36) **Systems thinking models** aim to analyse all the many feedback links that may help to explain why, for example, a community remains poor, or why a group of young people don't find work. These models have to use multiple disciplines and include practical as well as academic knowledge. At their best they give insights into where action can be most effective.

**End notes**

1. Lakhani, K. and Panetta, J. (2007) The Principles of Distributed Innovation. 'Innovations: Technology, Governance, Globalization.' 2:3 (Summer).
2. Chapman, J. (2002) 'System failure: why governments must learn to think differently.' London: Demos.
3. Bacon, N. *et al.* (2008) 'Transformers: How local areas innovate to address changing social needs.' London: NESTA.
4. Lerner, J. (2003) 'Acupuntura Urbana.' Rio de Janeiro: Editora Record.
5. Mulgan, G. *et al.* (2009) 'Sinking and Swimming: Understanding Britain's Unmet Needs.' London: The Young Foundation.
6. Shah, M.K., Degnan Kambou, S. and Monahan, B. (Eds) (1999) 'Embracing Participation in Development: Worldwide experience from CARE's Reproductive Health Programs with a step-by-step field guide to participatory tools and techniques.' Atlanta: CARE.
7. Hattie, J. (2008) 'Visible Learning: A synthesis of over 800 meta-analyses relating to achievement.' New York: Routledge.
8. For more information on statistical production techniques, see Deming, E.W. (1986) 'Out of the Crisis: quality, productivity and competitive position.' Cambridge, MA: MIT Press; or Deming, E.W. (2000) 'The New Economics for Industry, Government, Education.' 2nd ed. Cambridge, MA: MIT Press.
9. Pollak, V. (1990) Report to the Institute of Medicine, National Academy of Sciences, July; and Pollak V. and Lorsch J. (2001) Effective Computerised Patient Record Improves Patient Well-Being and Financial Performance. 'Dialysis and Transplantation.' Vol. 30, No.12, December 2001.
10. Fleck, F. (1979) 'Genesis and Development of a Scientific Fact.' Chicago: University of Chicago Press.
11. Nooteboom, B. (2000) 'Learning and Innovation in Organisations and Economies.' Oxford: Oxford University Press.
12. Laderman Ukeles, M. (2001) On Maintenance and Sanitation Art. In Finkelpearl, T. (Ed.) 'Dialogues in Public Art.' Cambridge, MA: MIT Press.

# 2 PROPOSALS AND IDEAS

## Finding the right answer

Asking the right question is the first step to finding the right answer. But once the right question has been framed, there are a series of methods for searching out and suggesting solutions. Some of these methods are specifically designed to encourage creativity and new ideas – such as competitions and prizes, online platforms and idea banks. Others are adapted from neighbouring fields, such as the arts and product design. There are also processes that encourage people and organisations to see and think differently, and institutions that play a key role in animating innovation by bringing in outside perspectives.

Ideas come from many sources, e.g. citizens, service users, communities, front line staff, other sectors, or other countries. In this section, we look at ways of tapping into these sources, and engaging citizens, users and others in the design and development of solutions.

As we have mentioned elsewhere, the way an innovation is developed is just as important as the innovation itself. The two are linked: the process will have an impact on the kind of innovation developed. In most cases the success of the innovation will rest on the participation and involvement of a wide variety of interests – the users and beneficiaries of the innovation as well as the producers and suppliers. In the case of the public sector, the engagement of the public in the formulation of policy is even more crucial because it is tied up with issues of trust, legitimacy and representation. This raises many questions about the nature and form of participation, e.g. what is the best way to engage and involve people?

## Imagining Solutions

There are a series of methods, especially within the field of design, which bring people together to develop solutions. Often this is called 'co-design'. Increasingly, some of these approaches are being used within the public sector to re-design services.

37)  **User-led design.** Users are often best placed to identify their own needs and come up with ideas about how best to meet them. In practice much of what is called 'user-led design' would be better described as 'user engagement in design', with designers and professionals still playing key roles as orchestrators and facilitators.

38)  **Re-designing services with users and producers** such as the work undertaken by design consultancies like IDEO, thinkpublic, Participle, and Live/Work or the Hope Institute's citizen teams formed around public service improvements. One recent example is IDEO's work with the SPARC centre at the Mayo Clinic (see-plan-act-refine-communicate), which involved turning an internal medicine wing into a laboratory designed to improve patient-provider experiences. The team turned an internal medicine wing into a 'four-zone journey' through which patients proceed: starting with the Service Home Base, moving to the Visitor-Facing Hub which leads to the Preparation Service Area before finally reaching Innovation Central. The wing is now a permanent section of the clinic where staff and doctors can develop and prototype new processes for improving service delivery. In another project, Hilary Cottam led a multidisciplinary team including prisoners, prison officers, prison managers and architects to develop a new collaborative design for prisons. The new design divides the prison up into houses – thereby maintaining security while allowing greater freedom of movement and freeing up financial and staff resources. The idea is to then refocus the prison day and the role of the prison officer around an intensive learning programme.[1]

39)  **Engagement of ex-users.** The Arizona Department of Corrections has involved recent prisoners in designing programmes to help others reintegrate into society.

40)  **Web-based tools for co-design,** such as the Australian site for people with disabilities and their carers, web2care.

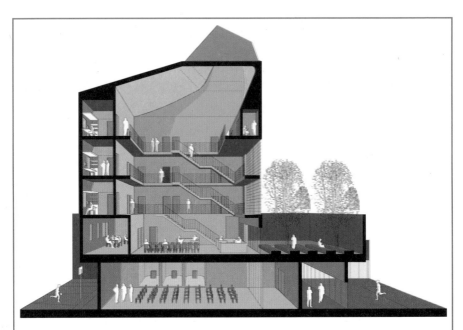

A Learning Prison. The prison is divided up into houses (the image above is a cross section) with cells on the top three floors, a communal space on the ground floor, and a learning centre in the basement. Image courtesy of Hilary Cottam, Buschow Henley, Do Tank Ltd.

41) **Creative thinking methods** such as Edward De Bono's 'Six Thinking Hats' and 'Lateral Thinking', and the work of consultancy firm What If?

42) **Forum theatre** is a form of theatre developed by Augusto Boal in Brazil, in which actors and non-actors play out stories of oppression (abusive husband mistreating his wife/factory owner exploiting the workers etc.). Boal called this and other types of participatory theatre, the 'Theatre of the Oppressed'.[2] In forum theatre, spectators can try to rewrite the story by stopping the performance at any time, and taking over from one of the actors playing the oppressed individual. If the other audience members do not think their suggestions are realistic they shout out 'magic' and someone else takes over.

Another technique used in the Theatre of the Oppressed is 'Image Theatre'. Spectators 'speak' through images; they make sculptures using

A Theatre of the Oppressed workshop in Philadelphia, USA, with Augusto Boal as the facilitator in the middle. Image courtesy of Morgan FitzPatrick Andrews.

participants' bodies to portray events and personal experiences. The idea is to get participants to reflect on particular issues, express their emotions and retell their experiences in order to develop new solutions. These sculptures can depict issues such as power relations – for example, those between husbands and wives, or between landowners and labourers. Or, spectators might choose to depict a more local problem like the lack of fresh water, or safety on public transport. This sculpture (which is called the 'actual image') is then used as a prompt for discussion about how the spectators themselves can change the situation. The participants rehearse this solution by moulding a new sculpture depicting the 'ideal image'.

43) **Continuous improvement methods** such as Toyota's Performance Management System, which aims to generate new ideas from frontline staff through quality circles. These are usually based on the idea that frontline staff have better knowledge about potential innovations than

managers or outsiders. Edward W. Deming, the pioneer of Toyota methods (also known as statistical production control, or 'statistical process control'), called for a system of management that was based on collaboration between management and staff – what he called, a system of 'profound knowledge'. This system consists of four interrelated aspects: appreciation of a system (understanding the overall processes involving suppliers, producers, and customers of goods and services); knowledge of variation (the range and causes of variation in quality, and use of statistical sampling in measurements); a theory of knowledge (the concepts explaining knowledge and the limits of what can be known); and knowledge of psychology (concepts of human nature).

Deming's 'Fourteen Points' also provides a blueprint for organisational transformation. These points include: create constancy of purpose towards improvement of product and service, with the aim to become competitive stay in business, and to provide jobs; cease dependence on inspection to achieve quality; eliminate the need for inspection on a mass basis by building quality into the product in the first place; and improve constantly and forever the system of production and service, to improve quality and productivity, and thus constantly decrease costs.[3]

44) **Quality circles** are a group of employees who volunteer to meet up to identify, analyse and solve work-related problems. They present their solutions to management who are then responsible for implementing these new ideas. The aim is to tap into the experience and insight of front line workers, who are often best placed to identify problems. This approach was pioneered by Toyota and plays an important step in their continuous improvement processes.

45) **Applying proprietary knowledge to social issues.** This method has been advocated by Mohammad Yunus because it uses the know-how and technology stored up in private firms to develop innovative solutions to problems related to poverty. The first example was the Grameen Danone partnership, bringing together Yunus' microcredit organisation and a leading French dairy products company to develop a new fortified yoghurt for low income consumers.

46) **Engaging citizens through media.** Direct media engagement in processes of social innovation is rare, but there are some examples. The UK TV station Channel 4 worked in Castleford engaging local residents in an experiment in urban redesign. Citizens were teamed up with

The new footbridge over the River Aire, designed by the citizens of Castleford as part of Channel 4 programme 'Big Town Plan'. Image courtesy of Stephen Bowler.

designers, architects and engineers to decide on regeneration priorities for Castleford. They were divided up into small working groups and each tasked with tackling one issue or area. Projects included the creation of a new footbridge over the River Aire; a gallery in the town centre; a play forest in Cutsyke; a new village green; and a new underpass into the town's shopping area. The Castleford Project is an excellent example of the power of television to lead to sustainable social change.

## Thinking differently

New solutions come from many sources – e.g. adapting an idea from one field to another, or connecting apparently diverse elements in a novel way. It's very rare for an idea to arrive alone. More often, ideas grow out of other ones, or out of creative reflection on experience. They are often prompted by thinking about things in new or different ways. Here, we outline some of the processes that can help to think and see differently.

47) **Starting with the user** through user research and participant observation, including ethnographic approaches such as user/citizen diaries, or living with communities and individuals to understand their lived worlds. SILK at Kent County Council, for example, used ethnographic research to review the lifestyles of citizens in their area.

48) **'Positive deviance'** is an asset-based approach to community development. It involves finding people within a particular community whose uncommon behaviours and strategies enable them to find better solutions to problems than their peers, while having access to the same resources. The Positive Deviance Initiative has already had remarkable results in health and nutrition in Egypt, Argentina, Mali and Vietnam.[4]

49) **Reviewing extremes** such as health services or energy production in remote communities. Design for extreme conditions can provide insights and ideas for providing services to mainstream users. For example, redesigning buildings and objects to be more easily used by people with disabilities has often generated advances that are useful to everyone.

50) **Visiting** remains one of the most powerful tools for prompting ideas, as well as giving confidence for action. It is common in the field of agriculture to use model farms and tours to transfer knowledge and ideas.

One excellent example is Reggio Emilia, a prosperous town in Northern Italy which, since the Second World War, has developed a creative, holistic and child-centred approach to early years' education which acts as an inspiration to early years' educators all over the world. Reggio Children is a mixed private-public company which co-ordinates tours and visits to early years' centres in the area.

51) **Rethinking space.** Many of society's materials, spaces and buildings are unused, discarded and unwanted. Old buildings and factories remain fallow for years, acting as a drain on local communities both financially and emotionally. The trick is to see these spaces and buildings in a more positive light, as resources, assets and opportunities for social innovation. Assets can be reclaimed and reused and, in the process, environments can be revitalised, social needs can be met, and communities energised. One example is the work of 'activist architect', Teddy Cruz. Cruz uses 'waste' materials from San Diego to build homes, health clinics and other buildings in Tijuana. He has become well-recognised for his low-income housing designs, and for his ability to turn overlooked and unused

2

Before. The old disused railway line in the Meatpacking district of Manhattan, New York City. Image courtesy of Benjamin Curry.

After. The old railway line has now been turned into Manhattan's first elevated park – the High Line. Image courtesy of Geoffrey Greene.

spaces within a dense, urban neighbourhood into a liveable, workable environment. Another example is the regeneration of Westergasfabriek by ReUse in Amsterdam, or the transformation of a disused elevated railway in New York into an urban park – the High Line.

## Open innovation

Open innovation describes the process of harnessing the distributed and collective intelligence of crowds. It is based on a number of principles, including: collaboration, sharing, self-organisation, decentralisation, transparency of process, and plurality of participants. The term was first used by Henry Chesbrough to describe a new model of product development-based on the free flow of information and ideas across departments and organisations.[5] It has taken on a wider meaning and application thanks to the internet, which has enabled large numbers of people to interact and participate at a relatively low cost.[6] Over the last few decades, there has been an explosion of methods designed to tap the public's imagination for ideas, perhaps in part a reaction against excessive deference to professions, and the idea that 'the expert knows best'. Many of these methods have been greatly helped by the ability of the internet to draw in a far wider range of people and ideas.

52) **Calls for ideas** involve asking a wide range of people to suggest ideas for strategy, projects, experiments, grantees or solutions to particular problems. There are a range of organisations which call for ideas: Social Innovation Camp, for example, launches a call for ideas to receive suggestions for projects in advance of its weekend-long events; Innovation Exchange use calls for ideas to solicit ideas for potential projects; and the European Commission launched a call for ideas for promoting intercultural dialogue across civil society in Europe in advance of the European Year of Intercultural Dialogue in 2008.

53) **Ideas marketplaces,** such as the World Bank's Development Marketplace which seeks ideas from development practitioners and their own staff, and then provides support to the winners.

54) **Competitions and challenges** can be an effective means of uncovering new sources of social innovation. They can also help accelerate the development of new solutions to social problems. Unlike the private market, however, competition is not always the driving force behind the development of new innovations in the social economy. This means

that competitions need to be structured in such a way that participants have the opportunity to collaborate, share and learn with each other. Examples include NESTA's Big Green Challenge and the various X-Prizes (see method 94 for more information on the Big Green Challenge and method 407 for X-Prizes).

55) **Ideas banks** were pioneered by the Institute of Social Invention in the UK. Its director, Nicholas Albery founded the Institute in 1985. Albery produced regular editions of the 'Book of Social Inventions' and the 'Book of Visions', and in 1995 he launched the Global Ideas Bank – an online repository of ideas and experiences – that has a database of 4,000 ideas online, receives a quarter of a million visitors a year, and, of those, 160,000 voted for one or more ideas. The Global Ideas Bank has helped spawn a number of similar websites, including the Norwegian Ideas Bank (which focuses mainly on issues of environmental sustainability) and Idea a Day (the top 500 ideas are published in the 'Big Idea Book', edited by the site's creator David Owen). Another initiative is My Health Innovation, a website which enables people to make suggestions for improving their healthcare systems. These websites include a vast range of ideas – everything from the brilliant to the downright absurd. But even when ideas are evidently excellent, there is no method for turning ideas into action.

56) **City ideas banks.** The lack of channels to develop ideas is the main weakness of ideas banks as a method for generating social innovation. However, ideas banks can be more closely tied into action. One successful example is the ideas bank launched by the Seoul Metropolitan Government in 2006. In 2007 it received 74,000 proposals (140 per day). Each entrant received a reply within a week. 1,300 ideas were adopted wholesale and many others in part. Examples of successful projects include setting up social enterprises, and lowering hand straps in the Metros for shorter passengers.

57) **Video booths** to capture the views and ideas of the public. Used at conferences, and in public spaces, to collect participants, views of the event and issues covered. YouTube can be used as a virtual video booth.

58) **Suggestion boxes** within organizations are the most basic method for soliciting innovations. Michael Young established a national suggestion box in 1968 as part of a programme to promote citizen-led innovation in public services.

*"I am too short to grab a handle in the subway. I need a lower handle".*
This is one of the ideas that was realised as a result of the Seoul Ideas
Bank. Image courtesy of the Hope Institute.

## Participation

Many governments, at every tier, are now trying to find ways of engaging the
public in shaping what they do, not just through elections every few years.
These methods are still being experimented with, and are as much about
creating a culture of openness to ideas as they are about generating ideas
themselves.

59) **Large scale government-led exercises** to involve the public in
generating ideas and possibilities, such as the Australia 2020 process
initiated by Prime Minister Kevin Rudd in 2008 to 'shake the tree' and
identify promising possibilities (including a thousand people gathering in
parliament for a weekend).

60) **Platforms for engaging citizens** such as the White House's new

The Citizen Summit III, convened in November 2003. More than 2,800 residents of the District of Columbia gathered on 15th November at the Washington Convention Centre to help plan the future of the city, discussing and voting on a range of policies. Image courtesy of AmericaSpeaks.

website, based on the principles as laid out in President Obama's Memorandum on collaborative, participatory and transparent government. The website enables citizens to take part in a discussion about the best way to effect the President's Memorandum in three stages – 'brainstorm', 'discuss' and 'draft' – which will culminate in new policy proposals. Other platforms such as MoveOn.org, MeetUp. org and Obama.com proved very effective during President Obama's election campaign in mobilising and galvanising grass roots support. These platforms are now providing the Obama Administration with mechanisms to solicit citizens' ideas and feedback.

61) **Methods for participation, idea generation and deliberation** such as the deliberative polling techniques developed by James Fishkin at the

These handheld devices allow participants to vote in real time. Image courtesy of AmericaSpeaks.

Center for Deliberative Democracy (Stanford University). This combines traditional public opinion research with intensive discussions in small groups to assess and advise on policy issues. Other examples include 21st Century Town Meetings, organised by AmericaSpeaks. These bring together between 500 and 5,000 people to discuss local, regional and/ or national issues. Participants are given electronic keypads and are able to vote in real time on various issues. They can also be divided up into small working groups.

62) **Processes for involving children** in generating innovations, decision making, urban design, planning, and school management. One example is the work of Children's Express in feeding children's views into the design of ideas for estate regeneration (and into influencing public policy – the Social Exclusion Unit commissioned children to interview other children living in housing estates to make presentations to ministers).

63) **'Wiki government'.** Using wikis to enable citizens to help draft policy. For example, New Zealand used a wiki to draft police legislation. The

wiki elicited thousands of contributions (some more constructive than others) and received up to 10,000 visits in one day.[7] Suggestions put forward included a governance board of eminent Kiwis, a minimum recruiting age for police, and a greater emphasis on victim's rights.[8] The review team judged the wiki to be very successful in raising awareness, bringing in new ideas and refining existing ideas.

64) **Participatory planning** or 'Planning for Real' pioneered by Tony Gibson, and other methods for involving the public in the design of solutions, mainly around urban design and architecture. Similar ideas have recently been adopted by the product design field.

65) **Parliamentary structures to develop citizen ideas,** like Korea's Tribunus Plebis, a committee of senior legislators committed to putting citizens' ideas into legislation.

66) **Citizen petitions** and other online platforms for capturing citizens' ideas on a range of matters including public service improvement. One example in the UK is the Prime Minister's e-Petitions website which has had nearly 10 million petitioners. The German parliament now encourages citizen petitions online. The petitioners who receive the most support get the chance to discuss their ideas in parliament – requiring radical innovation to parliamentary procedure. Another example is the people of Karelia petitioning for radical action on heart disease which led to the world's most innovative programme for public health.

67) **Citizen juries,** pioneered by the Jefferson Center in the US, bring a random selection of citizens together to assess the pros and cons of contested policy proposals, and sometimes generate new ideas. Citizen juries are usually established on a similar basis to judicial juries, but without any formal constitutional authority. These have been used across government in the UK – mainly in local government but also including the Department for Trade and Industry (now DBIS) and the Food Standards Agency.

68) **Citizen's panels** are similar to citizen juries but tend to involve more people – typically between 500 and 3,000 people. Participants are usually recruited by random sampling. Examples include Hackney's online citizen panel that covers a range of local issues including the quality of local service provision.

69) **Legislative theatre** is similar to forum theatre (see Method 42), but instead of acting out a scene where someone is being oppressed, the subject of the performance is a proposed new law. Spectactors can take to the stage, express their opinions and support, and oppose or modify any of the proposals. Augusto Boal developed this form of theatre while he was a councillor in Rio de Janeiro.[9] This was recently used in Brighton and Hove to promote public involvement in a health improvement programme.

## Facilitating participation

There are also a range of techniques – widely used in the developing world – for engaging participants in more effective and meaningful ways. Many meetings remain unproductive and uncreative they may not always be the place where new ideas first come into people's heads, but they play a crucial role in innovation. However they are decisive in shaping ideas and building support. Much attention is now being given to meetings to make them more effective – sometimes with much more open processes, sometimes with much more formal structures. Face to face meetings remain the most important in generating commitment to innovations, but increasingly technologies of all kinds are helping to transform meetings, enabling people to interact verbally, visually, and through simulations.

70) **Events and conferences for networking and learning** such as Poptech, TED (Technology, Entertainment, Design), and the Tällberg Forum hosted by the Tällberg Foundation, all share and spread information and examples of innovative practice. Most of these use fairly traditional formats, either workshops (for example, Tällberg) or short monologues (as in TED), but with plenty of time set aside for informal networking.

71) **Seedcamp** is a week-long event held every September in London to support 20 teams of young entrepreneurs. The event brings together a diverse 'mentor network' of serial entrepreneurs, corporates, product designers, venture capitalists, recruiters, marketing specialists, lawyers and accountants, that help the selected teams put together the foundations of a viable business.

72) **Virtual meetings** and conferences such as One World's parallel to Bali Conference on Climate Change, which was held in Second Life. Participants attend as a 'virtual' version of themselves (an avatar), and

Congressman Edward Markey (D-MA), Chair of the Select Committee on Energy Independence and Global Warming, speaks to the crowd at OneWorld.net's 'Virtual Bali' initiative on Second Life. Image courtesy of OneClimate.net/OneWorld.net.

engage as these selves in cyberspace.

73) **Webinars** are a fairly simple device for organising seminars over the web. Examples include the webinars organised by the Cities of Migration network which have linked NGOs, foundations and academics involved in social action related to diversity around the world.

74) **Dialogue Café** uses state of the art video conferencing (TelePresence) to link up citizens from all around the world. A person can go to a Dialogue Café in London, for example, and have a cup of tea with one friend sitting in a Dialogue Café in Lisbon and another in New York at the same time. This network of cafés will be opened up to non-profit organisations to host and organise events and meetings. Proof of concept cafés have been established in London, Istanbul and New York and the first five cafés (in London, Doha, Lisbon, Shanghai and Sao Paolo) will be operational in 2010.

75) **Open space events** (or 'unconferences') are participant driven – they

BarCamp Vancouver, 2009. Participants decide on the programme and run open, participatory workshops. In the photo above, a participant pitches her idea for a session. Image courtesy of flickr.com/photos/brycej.

decide on the programme and organise themselves into groups. Anyone who wants to initiate a discussion or activity pitches their idea to the whole group – those who are interested, join. The programme is fluid and changeable; nothing is set in stone as participants can move from one group to another, or start up a new group. One of the golden rules is that 'there are no spectators, only participants'. There are four principles for open space events: whoever comes are the right people; whatever happens is the only thing that could have; whenever it starts is the right time; and when it's over, it's over. One excellent example is BarCamp, a network of participant driven events. Initially, BarCamps focused on technology related issues but now cover topics as diverse as marketing and healthcare.

76) **Participatory workshops** are also known as Participatory Rural Appraisal (PRA) or Participatory Learning and Action (PLA). Robert

Chambers and others have developed a wealth of materials for organising and facilitating participatory workshops. These are meetings which enable local people to analyse, share and enhance their knowledge to plan, manage and evaluate development projects and programmes. Visual aids – such as mapping, videos, illustrations, timelines, card sorting and ranking, Venn diagrams, seasonal calendar diagramming and body maps are often used to engage participants and capture knowledge. They are often an effective means of getting participants to reflect on issues and their own personal experiences. These workshops also pay particular attention to group dynamics; breaking down distinctions between 'uppers' – those with power, standing, influence etc within a community – and 'lowers' – those with less power, influence and standing within a community. One of these activities is called Saboteur. The group divides into threes, with two as speakers and one as a saboteur. The speakers discuss a topic of their choice. The saboteur then interrupts, disrupts and distracts them. The speakers do not necessarily know that the third person is meant to sabotage their discussion. The group is then asked to reflect and discuss the experience.[10]

77) **Seating arrangements.** Group dynamics and levels of participation are also influenced by seating arrangements. There are some particularly effective methods for breaking down power imbalances and encouraging participants to take a full part in proceedings. These include circles, half circles and fishbowls. A fishbowl consists of an inner group of participants taking part in a discussion or activity. They are surrounded by a larger circle of participants. Those on the outer circle listen, observe and 'witness' the activity. Participants can take turns between sitting in the outer circle and sitting in the centre. Those on the outer circle can ask questions of those in the middle. Another technique is the Margolis wheel. This involves four to six pairs of chairs facing each other, arranged in a circle like a wheel. This exercise helps participants to realise that everyone has knowledge and experiences worth sharing (see p.48).

Another exercise is to ask participants to sit in a circle on the ground. This can subtly weaken or reverse power relationships. It is harder for one person to dominate without standing up, and if they do, they tend to exclude themselves from the task at hand. The power remains with those on the ground as they are the ones sorting the cards, drawing the maps, writing the notes, or placing the seeds to score the matrix. Quite literally, sitting on the ground is a good leveller; setting a tone which is open, collaborative and egalitarian.[11]

The Margolis Wheel. Participants are asked to reflect on a particular challenge or issue they face. Those sitting on chairs in the inner ring are 'counsellors' and those on the outer ring are 'clients'. The clients rotate after brief consultations with counsellors. When the outer ring has gone round once, they swap with those in the middle and become counsellors.

## Institutions

There are a range of organisations and multidisciplinary teams involved in the generation of workable ideas. Elsewhere, we look at institutions involved in all stages of innovation and across all sectors, but here we look at the innovation animators, those who can bring in different perspectives, and come up with innovative solutions.

78) **Think tanks** have a long established role in generating ideas. The UK Fabian Society is one of the oldest. Famous US examples include Brookings and the American Enterprise Institute. The most visible tend to focus on policy innovation. In the past, they acted as intermediaries between research done in universities and practitioners in government and elsewhere. The best think tanks can act as catalysts, combining research, policy ideas, and prompts for practical innovation in advance of policy change. A good recent example is Demos' work on the future evolution of personal budgets for recipients of care from government.

79) **Do tanks.** Some think tanks have moved towards a greater engagement with practice, recognising that practice is often ahead of theory, seeking

influence through practical demonstration rather than publications. The green movement is a particularly lively current space for new types of think tank and do tank, such as the New Economics Foundation and Forum for the Future.

80)   **Design labs.** In Finland, the national innovation agency SITRA has set up the Helsinki Design Lab, to see how design can be used as a strategic tool to tackle the complex and systemic challenges facing contemporary Finnish society. The Lab is currently organising an event to be held in September 2010 (based on previous events held in 1968 and 2008) to bring leading designers together with decision makers.

### End notes

1.   Cottam, H. *et al.* (2002) 'Learning Works: The 21st Century Prison.' London: Do Tank Ltd.
2.   See Boal, A. (1979) 'Theatre of the Oppressed.' London: Pluto Press; and Boal, A. (2002) 'Games for Actors and Non-actors.' London: Routledge.
3.   Deming, E.W. (1986) 'Out of the Crisis: quality, productivity and competitive position.' Cambridge, MA: MIT Press.
4.   Marsh, D.R., Schroeder, D.G., Dearden, K.A., Sternin, J. and Sternin, M. (2004) The Power of Positive Deviance. 'British Medical Journal.' Vol. 329, pp.1177-1179.
5.   Chesbrough, H. (2003) 'Open Innovation.' Cambridge, MA: Harvard Business School Press; and Chesbrough, H., Vanhaverbeke, W. and West, J. (Eds) (2006) 'Open Innovation: Researching a New Paradigm.' Oxford: Oxford University Press.
6.   See for example, Tapscott, D. and Williams, A.D. (2007) 'Wikinomics: How Mass Collaboration Changes Everything.' London: Penguin; Leadbeater, C. (2008) 'We-Think.' London: Profile Books; Surowiecki, J. (2004) 'The Wisdom of Crowds.' London: Little, Brown; and Von Hippel, E. (2005) 'Democratising Innovation.' Cambridge, MA and London: MIT Press.
7.   McCardle, H. (2008) 'Police Act Review: E-Communications Strategy.' Unpublished.
8.   McCardle, H. (2008) 'The case of the sneaky wiki.' Unpublished.
9.   Boal, A. (1998) 'Legislative Theatre: Using Performance to Make Politics.' London: Routledge.
10.   See Chambers, R. (2002) 'Participatory Workshops: a sourcebook of 21 sets of ideas and activities.' London: Earthscan.
11.   Ibid.

# 3 PROTOTYPING AND PILOTS

Once a promising idea has been proposed, it then needs to be tested in practice. Ideas develop through trial and error, and constant refinement. It's very rare for an idea to emerge fully formed. There are many methods in use for testing ideas out and refining them, ranging from the formal methods of randomised controlled trials to pilots and experiments. Social entrepreneurs often dive into practice and hope to learn quickly without using formal evaluations or tests. One of the common themes of contemporary social innovation is that it often works best by moving quickly into practice, rather than spending too long developing detailed plans and strategies. This section also looks at various funding tools for emerging ideas and prototypes.

## Prototypes, pilots and trials

As an idea progresses through multiple stages of rapid prototyping, it faces many challenges: the feasibility of making the product, delivering the service, how to deal with particular issues, what the economics look like, and how it could be made cheaper. The driving principles at this stage are speed, keeping costs low, tangibility and feedback loops from users and specialists.

81) **Prototyping** refers to the design of a working model of a product or service that can be used to test out the reactions of potential clients and providers. The concept comes from manufacturing, but is increasingly used to refer to services as well.

82) **Fast prototyping** emerged first in the software field, the idea being that faster implementation would speed up learning. This idea has now

spread into service prototyping and the social field – and organisations that aim to move quickly to put new ideas into practice (albeit on a very small scale) to learn quickly about what might work.[1]

83) **Slow prototyping** is only beginning to be used as a term to refer to situations where new capacities are necessary for a new model to succeed. Fast prototyping methods are bound to fail in such circumstances.

84) **Proof of concept testing** occurs before the prototyping stage and is a method for testing the idea – rather than the product or service. It usually involves asking members of the target audience to assess, rate and/or refine the product or concept.

85) **Beta testing** usually follows prototyping and concept testing and moves testing out to the users' actual environment for a 'real-world' test. The service/product is introduced to a small number of people who are then tasked with trying it out and reporting back any problems to designers and manufacturers.

86) **Partnership pilots** that bring together the public sector, philanthropists and NGOs to test out alternative models of provision. The work on eldercare by Atlantic Philanthropies in Ireland is a good example of this.

87) **Public pilots and experiments** use formal evaluation methods, and in some cases, controls. Pilots usually freeze a model for a period of time, and then measure its impact, sometimes in a number of different locations. Pilots are widely used – but can be too slow to cope with political and other pressures. They may also restrict evolution and learning because of the need to freeze the model to allow for formal evaluation.

88) **Randomised Controlled Trials** (RCTs) test a procedure within a randomly chosen sample of the public. In medicine, RCTs use 'double blind' methods so that the researchers don't know which users are receiving the treatment and which are receiving a placebo. RCTs have been increasingly used in fields such as welfare to work. They are often seen as a gold standard for evaluation, but can be unreliable – and are best used in conjunction with other research methods.

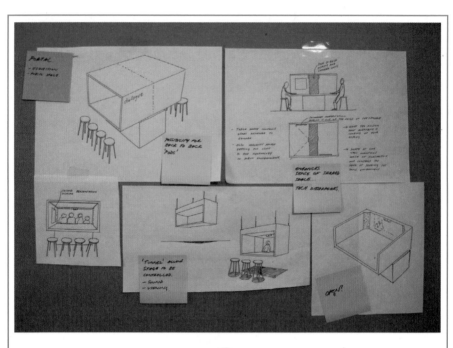

These are early sketches of the Dialogue Café TelePresence pods. Dialogue Café is a not-for-profit organisation which brings people together from all around the world in conversation through the use of TelePresence screens. Images courtesy of Dialogue Café.

89) **Whole System Demonstration Pilots** attempt to test out interconnected elements rather than the discrete services or actions usually associated with pilots. A good example is the current experiment for integrated health and social care through telecare, telehealth and other assistive technologies in Kent, Cornwall and Newham in the UK.

90) **Open testing** provides transparency during the testing stages. Examples include tracking the performance of different plug-in hybrid cars through Google, and C40 city governments. An example of open-testing, Google's initiative hopes to educate consumers body about the efficiency and cost-effectiveness of technology that is also environmentally friendly. The combination of social learning and technological advancement that open testing demonstrates has many applications in encouraging sustainable and systemic innovation that is both supply and demand driven.

This is one of Google's test cars. This fleet of hybrid plug-in vehicles is monitoring greenhouse gas emissions. Results are published online for public viewing. Image courtesy of Google, Inc.

## Finance for emerging ideas

A wide range of financial tools can be used at these early stages: small grants, convertible loans, to quasi equity, prizes, direct commissions, and tendering. Some of the most useful approaches link money to development.

91) **Grants and support for early ideas.** Finance for promising ideas usually takes the form of small grants for social entrepreneurs, or groups of front line workers, professionals, and citizens. Within universities the usual form is a grant, often with few conditions to allow a group of researchers to explore an idea without specifying outcomes. For external organisations, funding typically combines finance and some modest in-kind support (e.g. access to the skills of service designers). The staged funding provided by UnLtd in the UK is a good example.

92) **Small grants** aimed at community organisations and local groups, usually to shape and demonstrate innovations involving volunteers and/or community action.

93) **Challenge funds** within the public sector, like the Singapore Prime Minister's Enterprise Fund, or the UK's Invest to Save Budget. These are open to applications from existing public agencies, sometimes requiring that bids involve several different organisations dealing with 'joined up' problems or needs. Other examples in healthcare include the Innovation Challenge Prize which gives out £100 million to accelerate the development of innovative technologies, devices, and clinical procedures.

94) **Prizes and public challenges** can be an effective means of distributing funds and incentivising innovation. One of the traditional arguments in favour of prizes and competitions is the way in which it provides those giving out the prize a means of finding a solution to a problem without shouldering the burden of risk. Indeed, with competitions, it is the participants who are expected to foot the financial risk. In the social economy, however, there are arguments for sharing, rather than shifting, the risk. This can be achieved through a stage-gate process, where participants increase the level of investment as they pass through the various stages. This is how NESTA's Big Green Challenge was organised. It was launched in 2007 as a £1 million challenge prize fund to stimulate and reward community-led innovation in response to the threats posed by climate change. The Big Green Challenge, aimed at the not-for-profit

This is one of six hydroelectric systems being brought back to life by The Green Valleys. Image courtesy of Stephen Shepherd.

sector is the first challenge prize of its kind. Over a three stage process, competitors are supported to articulate, develop and, if they become a finalist, implement their ideas. The prize is awarded to one or more winners based on actual and projected ongoing performance at the end of the challenge's duration.

One of the finalists is the Green Valleys, a community interest company based in the Brecon Beacons in Wales. The Green Valleys hope to reduce carbon emissions, mitigate the risks of flooding and provide local residents with cheap, renewable energy. Through hydro, wind and thermal power (some of which will be community-owned) Green Valleys is hoping to make the 520sq mile area 'energy independent'. Excess energy will be sold back to the National Grid, generating a steady income stream for the company.

95) **Funding of networks** and requiring funding recipients to share emerging knowledge, as in the European Commission EQUAL programme, or the health collaboratives (the latter using structured

processes for sharing emerging innovations, and engaging diagonal slices of hierarchies).

96) **Funding for incubation.** Funding intermediaries to become specialist developers of promising ideas into workable forms, with a capacity to make follow on funding. Incubation includes several elements: scanning for elements from existing models, design, development, piloting, and business planning. The incubated concept can be sold to existing organisations or turned into a new organisation. A critical issue is to combine the investment decision and business support. Typical units for individual projects range from £2k-£250k, and the minimum size for incubation teams is around 10 people and 10 projects to ensure spread (see Part 2 for methods on incubation).

97) **In-house venturing capacities,** for example located in large NGOs and service organisations. These may be 'skunk works' or more like corporate venturing units whose primary target is the number of spin-off enterprises created.

98) **Paying for time.** Taking innovative front line workers out of service roles and putting them into incubators or prestigious time-limited roles to turn ideas into business plans (with the time costs then potentially turned into equity or loans).

99) **Vouchers** to provide purchasing power directly to NGOs or service providers to buy research in universities; or to club together to commission incubators (being tested by the ESRC).

100) **Collective voice and credits.** Allowing staff in an organisation to vote on which ideas and projects should receive early stage funding. This is a useful way of tapping collective intelligence and engaging a workforce in innovation.

101) **Funding public private social partnerships** on particular themes (such as reducing child poverty) and joint ventures – with a mix of grant funding or commissioning, or shared equity. The standard public private partnerships used to finance infrastructures and buildings have a mixed record in terms of value for money and success. But more imaginative partnerships directed to innovation look more promising.

102) **Direct commissions.** For example, a government department contracting for a new school curriculum or healthcare method through a direct contract with a preferred provider, sometimes with staged funding.

103) **Tendering for results.** For example, tendering for innovative approaches to cutting graduate unemployment or street homelessness, encourages bids by teams with the capacity to develop concepts to scale, by using a 'competitive dialogue' approach (as in the EU model).

104) **Creating new markets through procurement.** In cases where no established market exists for a particular service or technology, public procurement can create sufficient demand to establish entirely new markets for innovation. One example is the Internet, which was developed by DARPA (Defense Advanced Research Projects Agency) and took many years to commercialise (see Commissioning and Procurement, methods 170-183).

**End notes**

1. Dodgson, M., Gann, D. and Salter, A. (2005) 'Think, Play, Do: technology, innovation and organisation.' Oxford: Oxford University Press.

# 4 SUSTAINING

Only a minority of ideas will survive being tested and piloted. Even promising ones may simply not be sufficiently effective, or sufficiently cost-effective to survive. When an idea or cluster of ideas is new there are likely to be many competing alternatives. Usually just a few of these survive. Think, for example, of the bicycle or car, each of which took an extraordinary variety of forms in their first decades (from penny-farthings to three-wheelers) before a handful of variants became dominant.

Public feedback may be key, but evaluation methods also have a vital role to play since there is always an element of judgement in determining what counts as success or failure. The ability to judge innovations, and screen out a high proportion, is critical to the success of an innovation system. Trying to keep too many ideas alive may starve the best ideas of the resources they need to be sustained. We survey a wide range of assessment tools in the scaling section (see methods 208-229), since similar judgements need to be made as to whether an idea should be sustained or scaled.

For those that do pass through a period of successful prototyping and testing, launching a service or product on a sustainable basis involves the development of an economic model that will secure its financial future. That often requires changes to the idea itself: streamlining it; simplifying it; and/or turning into more modular elements so that it can work even without the enthusiasm of pioneers.

In the public sector, making an idea sustainable requires integrating the innovation into budgetary processes. That means evidence and tactics specific to the public sector. A service can sometimes be funded with new finance. At other times existing services need to be transformed or replaced. But to move from pilots and prototypes to a securely established public innovation, it is often advisable to set it up as a separate venture, with public finance and a service contract that can prove itself at scale. Indeed, this may be crucial if the new idea is to have the right culture and ethos.

Outside the public sector, sustaining an innovation will involve six key things:

- A business model that runs parallel to the core idea of the venture and which sets out how it can become sustainable.

- A governance model that provides a clear map of control and accountability, as well as protective safeguards (not least to protect it from predators if the project is a success).

- Sources of finance, both start-up capital in the short term and income streams over the longer term.

- A network and communications model to develop what we refer to as the venture's 'relational capital'.

- A staffing model including the role of volunteers.

- A development plan for operational systems – including management information, reporting and financial systems, IT, supply chain systems and systems for risk management.

These will be translated into an economic or business plan, which details the service or initiative, how it will be provided, by whom, with what inputs, how much it will cost, and how it will generate income.

Tensions are bound to emerge at this stage. Any venture driven by a social mission has an interest in maximising the spread of an innovation beyond the level dictated by the venture's own financial interest. This raises a tension between an interest in collaborating and sharing ideas on the one hand, and an interest in restricting information to safeguard the financial survival of the organisation on the other.

Most social ventures have to do both – to remain open and collaborative, while surviving financially. It is this very openness and readiness to share information and know-how that often generates income in roundabout ways. It is also this openness, together with the social mission of the venture, that attracts voluntary contributions in terms of volunteer time, resources, and donations. Social ventures have much to gain from keeping open, yet this is easier said than done. Ventures are subject to the day to day disciplines of keeping the show on the road. They tend to turn inwards behind their organisational moat. The idea pulls one way, the daily practice another.[1]

## Creating a business

Turning a good idea into something sustainable outside of the public sector depends on a business model – a clear idea of how it will generate a sufficient income stream that covers more than costs. Effective supply and effective demand need to be brought together. Effective supply means that whatever is being provided has been shown to work and to be cost-effective. Effective demand refers to the willingness of someone to pay for what's on offer, which may be a public agency or the public themselves.

105) **Innovative business models.** The business concepts of the social economy require as much care and creativity in their generation as the social ideas. The two are best developed together to sustain and re-enforce each other. For social enterprises, the business model represents a strategy for sustainability. It needs to be simple, persuasive and striking, since along with the social idea, it is a key part of a venture's attraction. Business models that work are themselves a prime area for social innovation. They are as diverse as business models in commercial markets, ranging from direct service provision to commissioners, through models that create value for customers to models similar to those around the web that share knowledge and intellectual property.

106) **Business strategies.** The context for a business model is a business strategy about how the proposed venture is positioned on the economic field of play. There will be key points of control in any sector of production. In some it is retailing and distribution; in others it is a key stage in processing; or in knowledge management systems; or the control of a key input such as a critical site or personnel (as in sport). Mapping a sector will suggest the points at which a new social venture has the best chance of success, and of influencing the way the sector works.

107) **Incomes and outcomes.** There are a range of social business models that involve recognising the potential value of a venture's assets and

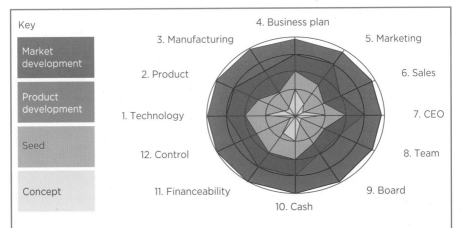

In the diagram the most progress has been made along the technology axis (as we might expect in Silicon Valley), along with the business plan, the CEO and the financing axes. The least developed are sales, the team, the Board, and systems of control. For the social economy the issues of control, the team and relations with users are likely to have greater priority, and may in fact be the substance of a new social technology on which a venture is based. In the diagram below we identify 12 alternative axes which may be more appropriate for social ventures.

**4**

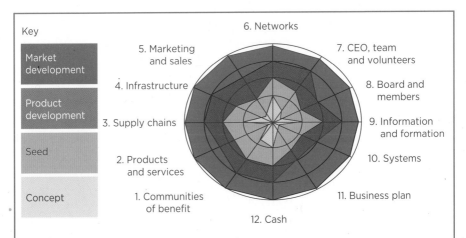

These are useful tools, both for managers and investors, that drive attention to the many elements that combine to make a business work – any one of which could be the decisive weakest link.

disaggregating its activities to generate alternative income streams. Particularly instructive for social ventures are the lessons from the business models adopted by web companies which, like social ventures, have an interest in maintaining free access, while at the same time generating revenues indirectly as the result of the response that the free service attracts.

108) **Business plans.** Business models together with business strategies then need to be turned into business plans. Although it is rare for a social venture to be a straightforward implementation of a blueprint (it is much more like a process of discovery and unfolding), plans help to clarify tasks, milestones, and sequencing – for example of investment in people, equipment and market growth. Business plans cannot design the future, and few survive their first encounters with reality. But they provide a chart for a venture's theatre of operations and demonstrate the competence of those engaged in taking the venture forward.

109) **Business plan assessment methods.** There are many methods that help to define business models and business plans. The Bell-Mason methods from the field of venture capital, for example, provide a rigorous framework for paying attention to the many elements that together make up a credible business plan, such as skills, marketing, and finance. Their model for new ventures has 12 axes shown in the diagram below. For each of them, progress is mapped in four stages. First is the concept stage. This is seeded and then developed as a product. Finally there is the market development stage. They have used this diagnostic model to chart the progress of more than 450 ventures, in order to identify key areas for further development.

## Ownership and organisational form

There comes a point when every venture has to decide what organisational form to take, what kind of decision making and accountability processes to adopt, and which kinds of information and financial management systems to put in place. These decisions can be costly and time consuming. But getting it right early on provides structures and systems which act as skeletons that help hold the organisation together. Forms of ownership set out rules related to an organisation's mission, its governance structures, and how its yield is distributed. But ownership can also be how a project mobilises support, encouraging a sense in others that the project is theirs.

In the social economy, ownership is an ambiguous concept. Its organisational structures are the site of contending pressures of goals and interests. The organisation may have a social goal of benefitting others, but to do so it involves those with some measure of private interests – finance, staff, suppliers, and purchasers. Some may exercise their interests at arm's length – and their market or financial power may be such as to reduce the social project to little more than a sub-contractor or agent, severely restricting the autonomy of the owners. But others may seek closer involvement in the project's direction. How can the forms of ownership and governance accommodate these pressures and turn them to good account?

110) **Informal structures** such as those used by Un Techo para Chile, which was set up in 1997 to provide decent housing for some of Chile's poorest citizens. Under the programme, recent graduates and young professionals spend two years working on various projects, building houses, and turning slum dwellings into safe and decent homes. The organisation has now spread across South America, enlisting hundreds of

Some of those involved in building houses and turning slum dwellings into safe and decent homes. Image courtesy of Un Techo para Chile.

Just a few of the houses built by Un Techo para Chile (A Roof for Chile).
Image courtesy of Un Techo para Chile.

thousands of volunteers to build over 40,000 homes. By 2010, they hope
to build a further 10,000 homes across the continent. Until recently, Un
Techo para Chile had no legal status – it was simply a loose network
of students, young professionals, and residents. Felipe Berríos, who
launched the initiative, believed that this was the best arrangement –
it allowed the volunteers to have ownership over the project and also
meant that Un Techo para Chile could not be sued by landowners. In
2005, Un Techo para Chile began to collaborate and work with the
government to provide housing on government land. In order to do so,
they had to become legally constituted. Another example is Alcoholics
Anonymous (AA), which is organised as a membership network rather
than a formal organisation in order to prevent bureaucracy.

111) **Private companies.** For some social ventures, simple private company
models are the most suitable: they may help with raising equity, and
they can formalise the contribution of a small group of founders. Their
limitation is that the founder's influence tends to decline over time
(as new capital is brought in), and they cannot be indefinitely tied to a
mission or a set of values. Most social ventures depend on restrictions

to dividends and/or to the terms of exit as key design features to ensure investors place the venture's values before maximising financial returns.

112) **Adapted private companies.** Corporate forms can be adapted to reflect values and different models of accountability, for example by creating different categories of shareholder; by giving particular groups voting rights; or golden shares. These arrangements can be fixed through the constitution, a shareholders' agreement, or the terms of a limited partnership.

113) **Limited Liability Partnerships** are a form of legal ownership that gives the benefits of limited liability, but allows its members the flexibility of organising their internal structure as a traditional partnership. It has been used by housing associations and local authorities together with private developers in order to deliver low cost home-ownership/equity share and social housing – for example the L&Q Group and George Wimpey in Academy Central, Barking. It is also the form adopted by Riversimple, a project to prototype an electric car.

114) **Co-ops and Associations** tend to be less flexible than private companies, but also more resilient. Clubs, mutual insurance companies, and friendly societies all have an associative form. Their defining purpose is the interests of their members, as consumers, or workers, or participants, but their culture is social, are committed to the communities in which they operate, providing work, services, and support. Examples include Japanese food consumer co-ops, and the Mondragon family of co-ops in Spain.

115) **Mutuals.** Co-ops are one type of mutual. Mutuals have taken many forms in the past with finance as a particularly important sector. More recently they have become significant in utilities, with Welsh Water as a large and successful example, as well as in sport, where there are now 15 football or rugby clubs under the ownership or control of supporters' trusts, with a further 95 supporters' trusts having shareholdings in their clubs. There has also been a growth of 'New Mutualism', which has been promoted, with government support, as a way of democratising public services. There are now 125 NHS Foundation Trusts that have been established as multi-stakeholder mutuals; GPs have organised mutuals to provide out of hours primary care; there has been a growth of publicly funded childcare co-ops, as well as leisure trusts and social enterprises running public leisure facilities. There are now 109 such leisure mutuals

A Working Rite match – Craig with his tradesman-mentor Keith. Image courtesy of Working Rite.

**4**

with a combined annual turnover of £640 million. In education, there has been a parallel development of co-operative foundation schools. Fifteen co-operative trusts covering 25 schools have already been established, with discussions under way with a further 60 schools. As of 2009, there are 23 million members of mutuals in the UK, ranging from the long established retail and financial co-ops, friendly societies, insurers, building societies, and housing associations, to the new mutuals and community trusts that have grown so markedly over the last decade.

116) **Partnerships.** Memorandums of understanding can formally express a convergence of will between two parties in cases where it would be impossible to form a legally binding agreement. If the relevant incentives of law enforcement are appropriate then operational contracts can be written and signed.

117) **Charities** are the legal form that puts the organisation's mission first, with the requirement to provide public benefit as the condition for the various benefits of charitable status, including tax benefits.

118) **Community Interest Companies.** This is a new legal status for social enterprises, and is similar to charitable status. CIC status enables social ventures to access equity investment while maintaining the social goals of the enterprise as paramount. They do this by having a lock on assets and a cap on dividends, which partially insulates the enterprise from the private market's imperative for profit maximisation and capital growth. One example is Working Rite, which specialises in work-based mentoring projects. Based on the idea that 'everyone remembers their first boss', Working Rite matches an unemployed young person with a skilled tradesman and supports the young person through a six month apprenticeship. As of late December 2009 there were 3,261 companies registered as CICs.

## Governance

Ownership structures bring with them important dynamics that may help or hinder the organisation in realising its mission. The best forms of ownership and governance reinforce relational capital, creating a source of resilience for when the enterprise goes through difficult times.

119) **Boards** are one of the key design features of any organisation. As instruments of governance of social ventures, they have a dysfunctional history. They represent a division between moral and manual labour, between the board that interprets the social goals of the organisation and the staff who carry them out. Yet the success of a social venture depends on an integration of the two. The means of overcoming this division is in part through participation in an active process of formation, and in part through the engagement of board members in the active work of the venture. Boards are legally required to act as guardians of values and mission, and often see themselves as having to resist innovation. But increasingly social ventures are seeking ways to involve stakeholders that do not depend on representation on a board.

120) **Boards for innovation.** Some design features of boards can actively promote innovation. In principle, user and beneficiary representation on management boards can serve as a channel for new ideas from the front line. Similarly, boards can appoint members to act as champions of innovation in the organization ensuring that there is a pipeline of innovations being developed.

121) **Membership involvement** can be tokenistic and cosmetic or a

significant source of engagement and capital. Most businesses see AGMs as an annoying necessity where small shareholders can vent their anger. Social movements, by contrast, use AGMs to reinforce commitments to the mission.

122) **Stakeholder governance.** There are a number of ways in which core stakeholders can be incorporated in the structure of an organisation and its processes. These include the constitution, a shareholders' agreement, or the terms of a limited partnership.

123) **Open guides.** The social sector has started to develop more comprehensive guides to help ventures make decisions about governance models and organisational forms. These can be used at an early stage to guide negotiations between stakeholders. We anticipate considerable web-based innovation in this field, with websites providing guidance on organisational forms, and governance. One interesting example is One Click Organisations, an ultra simple web-based tool for creating new organisations, changing constitutions, and engaging members and stakeholders.

124) **Consumer shareholding** can be used to involve consumers more directly in the work of a venture, both directly, and through representation on the board. This was one of the main reasons Cafédirect opted to have a share issue geared to small shareholders as a means of raising finance.

125) **Gold Standards and Golden Shares.** Social businesses like Cafédirect have adopted a detailed Gold Standard to provide a constitutional anchor to the company's social character, and have a separate company of Guardians to ensure that the gold standard is maintained. More common has been the use of Golden Shares, for example by government to safeguard the public interest in a privatised company. The Share may ensure that the number of shares taken by one investor is limited, or constraints are placed on the disposal of assets. Golden Shares may also carry with them the right to appoint a member to the company's board.

## Organisation and management models

126) **Hierarchical organisations committed to social purposes.**
Much of the social economy is made up of organisations that are not dissimilar to those in the state or private business which have a

pyramid structure with authority flowing downwards and accountability flowing upwards. In charities the trustees sit at the top, above the chief executive. Hierarchies have survived because they are effective and well understood models.

127) **User orientation and autonomous work groups.** Large commercial organisations have moved away from hierarchical organisations to models where there are relatively autonomous groups of front line staff, supported by the technical staff, and management. Control is exercised by the users/consumers and their requirements, translated through information and operational systems that highlight the degree to which consumer demand is being successfully met. The demands of a 'Just in Time' system of production, for example, provide the structure and discipline to front line staff formerly supplied by hierarchical managers. The manager's task in this case is to assess variances in performance and ensure the system is integrated effectively. This thinning of hierarchies and distributing of responsibility to front line teams has been termed 'heterarchical' where there are many nodes of power and responsibility. Another version is provided by Visa (jointly owned by its member banks) which developed what its founder Dee Hock called a 'chaordic' organisation, combining organisation and chaos. For social innovation, such models are particularly applicable to large charities and to public services.

128) **Distributed organisations.** Many social ventures try and avoid strict hierarchical structures by remaining small and by subdividing (like cells) or collaborating with other similar ventures. Some have adopted a franchised model, to allow each unit to remain relatively small, while benefitting from economies of scale for the group of ventures as a whole. This is the basis for the expansion of Riverford Organic Vegetables Ltd, which franchises distributors of it's organic produce, while involving 12 sister farms in a co-operative of regional producers. This structure was intentionally adopted by the founder of Riverford, Guy Watson, to keep his venture small, and production local. The resulting network now delivers 47,000 organic food boxes a week.

129) **Dimensions of management.** Different development stages of the innovation will require different forms and styles of leadership and management. In the initial stages, leadership is that of a pioneer. As the organisation develops, leadership needs to take on the skills of adapting, listening, and learning. Management is not only about the

giving of orders, but it is about seeding multiple centres of activity and initiative, and building forums to allow this mosaic of energy to interact – channelling debate and tension into further innovation.

130) **Managing systems and structures to maintain innovation.** There is commonly a tension between the demands of continuing operations and the venture's ability to maintain innovation. The financial and managerial demands of innovation may put pressure on existing business. There are different management styles that may be appropriate for innovation and operations. Spin-offs are one way of managing this tension. Careful succession planning is another, permitting the initial innovators to move on to new tasks.

## Operations

The distinctive value and values of a social venture show up not just in its structures but in its operations – how it works with others, uses technologies or works in partnership.

131) **Socially-oriented supply chains.** Transparent supply chains that reflect the values of the venture are often a key element in sustaining and expanding a social venture. An organic food box scheme, for example, depends on its certified supply chain. A fair trade company may benefit farmers, but it also needs to avoid processing in plants with poor labour records. It often takes time to build up robust supply chains of this sort, but once established they need to be maintained with as much care as Japanese assemblers give to their different levels of supply.

132) **Socially-oriented demand chains.** For some ventures providing intermediate goods or services the challenge is how to develop a demand chain that processes or distributes the good or service. The community movement for recycling worked with local and regional governments to promote processing factories – and in some cases industries – to use the materials that they had collected. They explored new uses for recovered material like glass, or developed multiple grades of compost to meet different types of demand. Sometimes the chain may be closely linked. Farmer's co-ops in Italy for example, supply co-operative processing factories, who sell through co-operative shops, and are funded by co-operative banks. But as with supply chains, the goal is to have the demand chain reflecting the social mission of the venture.

133) **Shared backroom economies.** Many new ventures carry high overheads because of their small scale, or they fail to invest in financial and operational systems that are important for their effective working. It is important for ventures to find ways of sharing these overheads, or access part-time specialists, or download systems (such as web designs and technologies) that are becoming freely available. One model is the consortia developed by the small Italian firms in the 'Third Italy'. CNA, the umbrella body for artisan producers, provides collective services such as booking, accounting, legal advice, and even political representation to its federated artisans.

134) **Collaborative technologies.** It is often important for ventures to adopt technologies that are flexible, adaptable, and suitable for distributed activity. The Grameen-Danone partnership developed micro yoghurt plants (in spite of the initial scepticism of the machine designers) that enabled easy access to the women distributing the yoghurt to the villagers, and avoided the high costs of refrigeration.

4

Micro – yoghurt factory in Bogra, Bangladesh. Image courtesy of Danone Communities.

A training session for the women who will sell the yoghurt. Image courtesy of Danone Communities.

'Grameen Ladies' meet with representatives of Danone to learn about the product and possibly become sellers of this product. Image courtesy of Danone Communities.

Roshonara, a 'Grameen Lady', selling Shokti Doi yoghurt, door to door. She sells approximately 70-100 cups of yoghurt a day. She is able to supplement her household income by about 17 dollars a month. Her husband is a rickshaw driver making less than 100 dollars a month. Image courtesy of Danone Communities.

Some of the children enjoying Shokti Doi. Image courtesy of Danone Communities.

## Relational capital

New ventures put much of their energy into securing financial capital – money to invest in fixed assets on the one hand, and working capital on the other. But relational capital is just as important. This is both the knowledge and trust built up between a venture and its users and suppliers, and the relationships between a venture and its staff and volunteers. Conventional accounting takes little account of this intangible capital, yet in all social ventures it is the foundation of their strength, and of their distinctiveness.

We use the concept of relational capital to capture the quality of relationships within which economic exchanges take place. This is the issue of greatest relevance for a social venture, as its fortunes depend on the range and depth of its relationships that.

These relationships are multifaceted. They include the nature of its connections: to users and investors; to suppliers and distributors; and with its own staff, board and volunteers. With many of them there will be formal agreements, but whereas in the private market economy relationships take place across a territory demarcated by the interests and boundaries of private property and contract, for a social venture the boundaries are more porous – internal and external interests mesh.

It is one of its greatest potential assets that a social venture can attract support and resources from outside itself, as well as motivation from within, on the basis of its ideas and the way it works to realise them. This creates particular issues for management.

135) **Keeping it 'open'.** Investing in human resources to ensure a social venture's openness is as important as investing in a building or machine. For it concerns the formulation and presentation of a venture's identity, to itself, and to the outside world. Visits from external experts can be an aid to training and formation or, as in the case of SEKEM, they can keep an organisation open to new ideas and models. The quality and extent of a project's external relationships should be thought of as a cultural project, for it is from an open and inclusive culture that a social venture draws much of its strength.

136) **Systems for user feedback** to keep users at the centre. Social ventures tend to rely on their idea to galvanise funders and users. They place their operational focus more on supply than demand. But

to ensure that the venture remains generative rather than static, users should remain central – a service should know who they are and who is missing, how the service is used and perceived, and how it could be improved and added to. Just as no venture can operate without a finance and accounting system, it requires a system of user relationships and feedback as part of its operational spine.

137) **Web presence.** All social ventures now have to have a website. But their full potential has only begun to be explored. Many ventures are by their nature information intensive – in respect to the quality and tangibility of their work, the stories of those involved in it, and the range of people with whom it interacts. It has therefore become crucial for ventures to have access to the tools – wikis, chat rooms, forums, comment boxes, and blogs. It also needs high quality design to ensure usability and navigability, ways of connecting each web site to others (through links and RSS feeds) as well as establishing a presence on other social networking sites like YouTube and Facebook which can act as feeders to the venture's website. Above all, a venture needs to devote resources to the constant updating and active hosting of their sites. A good example is the site of the co-operative football team Ebbsfleet United (My Football Club), which has a team of six working on their website to involve the members, a model that could be adopted by many consumer co-ops among others.

138) **Marketing and branding.** Social ventures, particularly those that are tax-funded or grant-aided, have been suspicious of branding. Governments find themselves criticised for spending money on branding. Grant givers are reluctant to fund expenditure on brands and all that is involved in developing them. But all ventures have an appearance and a style. It is part of the way they communicate. Social ventures should see branding as a flame that indicates a presence and attracts people towards it. It is the first step in widening its connections.

139) **A working museum.** A workplace should provide a clear and engaging insight into the work that goes on and culture that rests within the organization. Some ventures go further and make their workplace into a working gallery or museum. They demonstrate much of their work visually, through photos and graphs. Some arrange tours and generate income from them. For example, Vauban in Freiburg, Germany, and Bo01 in Malmo, Sweden, are examples of low-carbon communities which allow visitors to touch, use and see the results, as well as see the work of the employees and staff. It is always a useful exercise for a venture

This is a view of the Vauban development in Freiburg, Germany. It is one of the world's leading 'eco-towns'. In the early 1990s, the local government mandated that all new construction must be sustainable. Here, solar power is used to heat homes and provide electricity. The town is a showcase for low-energy, sustainable housing, attracting visitors and investors alike. Image courtesy of Rolf Disch, SolarArchitecture.

to consider how it could best present its work and its social purpose tangibly as if it were a gallery.

140) **Open events** to provide an opportunity for organisations to engage a wide variety of people in the work of the organization. They are an occasion for experiencing the venture's culture. Events of this kind are much more important for social ventures than commercial ones. They allow a wider group to share in the spirit of the venture.

141) **Open forms of intellectual property** to maximise the spread and diffusion of the idea or service. Social ventures have an interest in adopting open forms of intellectual property. They stand to benefit from a shared commons of knowledge, both in what they receive back from a reciprocal economy of information, and in extending the value and impact of the knowledge they contribute. BioRegional (the social

venture that initiated the zero carbon development at BedZed) recently placed its most valuable technical information on the web for open access in order to enable its ideas to be adopted more rapidly. Open access or open licensing allows people to build on a venture's knowledge assets, and to mix together these assets with others. For some ventures this may involve the foregoing of possible income streams from the sale of that knowledge, but there are many alternative means of generating income, not least through the strengthening of the venture's relational capital through a policy of open information.

142) **Formation for developing skills and cultures.** The formation or training and shared orientation of those engaged in the venture plays a critical role in providing cohesion to social ventures. It informs the articulation of the venture's central purpose. It provides meaning for those working for the venture, for investors and volunteers, and it gives to the venture a living, reflexive power that is not limited to particular individuals or levels in the organisation, but to all those involved. This is important also, for public innovation, through, for example, bodies like the National School of Government (NSG) and the Improvement and Development Agency for local government (IDeA), CELAP in China, or the Australia and New Zealand School of Government (ANZSOG).

143) **Values-based policies for people and pay.** Developing its staff is important, not only for the venture itself, but to create a group of individuals able to put the ideas into practice more widely. Its internal policies, the structures of pay, and its operational practices should reflect the venture's mission, and avoid the tensions that can arise between market rates of pay and what is considered equitable with respect to all staff, volunteers, and the venture's beneficiaries.

144) **Valuing the voluntary.** In a volunteer economy, roles, relationships and incentives have to be thought about differently to those where there is a contractual wage relationship. If the volunteer receives no payment, then the experience of the work and of contributing to a social goal has to be powerful enough to persuade them to continue. This requires particular managerial and organisational skills, and some overhead expense, but there is great potential value to a new venture if it makes one of its goals the attraction and effective employment of a wide range of volunteers. Many organisations, like the social housing venture Habitat for Humanity, are primarily volunteer organisations of this kind, with simple goals and a strong ethos.

## Venture finance

Every innovation process requires some finance. For social ventures it is key that the sources of finance should share the venture's social goals as the primary driver of the enterprise. This may not always be possible. Raising capital may involve some compromise with the providers of capital, but the goal should always be to find ways for the core finance to come from those who share the venture's mission.

As a rule, the earlier stages require the least money, but they are also the hardest point at which to raise money. Here we look at the financing tools that help to take an idea from initial pilots into more sustainable operation. To finance new ventures there are a range of ethical banks and social funding agencies devoted to supporting new and expanding ventures. All forms of finance bring with them power relationships, which can sometimes threaten the values and relationships which the venture is built on. To guarantee that the initial venture funding remains subordinate to the values of the social mission, enterprises can raise social equity, limit the quantity of common shares, and seek subordinated loans from sources ready to share early risk without demanding a counterbalancing share in the project's equity.

145) **Grant funding** is sometimes provided to grow social ventures. This usually depends on one or two wealthy philanthropists having a sufficient commitment to the project. A good example is the philanthropic support provided for Australia's Inspire, firstly to establish itself in that country, and then to expand to the USA.

146) **Loan finance.** Where there is a clear future income stream, loans are often the best form of finance. There are distinct forms of lending within the social economy that include saving and lending circles, but much of the loans now being made for social ventures are coming from specialised social finance organisations, sometimes seeking security (usually from property), and sometimes lending against contracts. There are different loan finance options depending on organisational form (for charities, Community Interest Companies, spinouts, private firms). They include loans for working capital; capital acquisition loans (e.g. property); risk capital (e.g. underwriting fund-raising efforts, or seeking new contracts); factoring – linked to contract values; and loan guarantees (unsecured) – typically 70-85 per cent guarantees. Loan provision for social projects is now a reasonably mature industry in many countries with typical unit scales from £25k-£500k.

147) **Equity** is likely to be invested into both creating and growing enterprises, and supporting spin-outs from the public sector. It can be used for various kinds of social enterprises as well as for-profits. The forms used will include: quasi-equity – which can be royalty based, or profit based; convertible loans – converted to equity linked to trigger points (for example, first equity funding round or turnover targets); and equity with full rights. Typical units: £100k-£5 million, alongside debt.

148) **Crowdfunding.** Instead of raising funds through banks and other intermediary institutions, the web opens up the possibility of making new types of connections and raising finance from potential consumers. This is how My Football Club raised enough capital to purchase Ebbsfleet United.

149) **Public share issues** are most suitable at times of expansion, when the enterprise has proved itself, and risks are reduced. They sometimes have an advantage over venture capital funding in that they can tap investors who want to make social impact their primary incentive rather than financial returns.

4

Here is one of Britain's few co-operatively owned wind farms at Westmill in Oxfordshire. It has 2,400 shareholders. Image courtesy of Andrew Watson.

150) **Social Impact Bonds** are a financial tool being developed in the UK to provide a new way to invest money in social outcomes. Government agrees to pay for measurable outcomes of social projects, and this prospective income can then be used to raise bond financing from commercial, public, or social investors. This is possible where outcomes are measurable and lead to tangible public financial savings. Social Impact Bonds could play a particularly important role in financing preventative programmes, though it remains unclear how much they will be used primarily to spread already proven models (with reasonably reliable risk) or whether they will be used to finance innovation (see also method 368).

151) **Venture philanthropy** uses many of the tools of venture funding to promote start-up, growth, and risk-taking social ventures. It plays an important role in diversifying capital markets for non-profits and social purpose organisations. The field is small but maturing. Organisations include BonVenture in Germany, Impetus Trust and Breakthrough in the UK, d.o.b. foundation in the Netherlands, Good Deed Foundation in Estonia, Invest for Children (i4c) in Spain, Oltre Venture in Italy, and both Social Venture Partners and Venture Philanthropy Partners in the US.

## Sustaining innovations through the public sector

Sustaining ideas in the public sector involves different tools to those needed in markets or for social ventures. There are similar issues of effective supply (the proof that a particular model works) and effective demand (mobilising sources of finance to pay for the idea or service).

152) **Business cases within the public sector.** In some parts of the public sector the language of the 'business case' has been adopted. This means outlining how the innovation will meet targets and goals more cost-effectively than alternatives.

153) **Public policy.** One strategy is to integrate the innovation into public policy, at either national or local level – for example, the commitment to extended schools in the UK in the late 2000s – which then translates into funding, targets and other tools for putting it into practice, using the full range of policy tools.

154) **Public programmes.** An innovation can be sustained by being part

of a public programme that has funding attached to it. This is how innovations in early years' provision, such as Headstart and SureStart, were funded.

155) **Public regulations,** such as regulations requiring a particular type and scale of play area in urban developments, can also provide the pull-through that is needed to sustain innovations.

**End notes**

1. See Murray, R., Caulier-Grice, J. and Mulgan, G. (2009) 'Social Venturing.' London: NESTA.

# 5 SCALING AND DIFFUSION

## Generative diffusion

According to former US President Bill Clinton, "nearly every problem has been solved by someone, somewhere. The challenge of the 21st century is to find out what works and scale it up". There are many methods for growing social innovations – from organisational growth and franchising to collaboration and looser diffusion. Some of these involve scaling – a metaphor taken from manufacturing. Others are better understood as more organic – 'cut and graft', with ideas adapting as they spread, rather than growing in a single form. Indeed, most social ideas have spread not through the growth of an organisation but through emulation. The supply of ideas and demand for them tend to co-evolve: there are relatively few fields where there are straightforward solutions, which can simply be spread.

There are marked differences in the spread and diffusion of innovations between the social and market economies. The private economy is structured to reserve the benefits of an innovation to its own organisation or to those licensees or franchisees willing to pay for it. The social economy – being primarily oriented around social missions, favours the rapid diffusion of an innovation, rather than keeping it private. This is one reason why the social economy has less compulsion to organisational growth and more towards collaborative networking as a way of sharing innovation.[1]

As a result of these differences, the spread of a social innovation tends to be a more complex flow-like process of interaction and modification. It is analogous to the spread of a chemical liquid. It has been termed fission, contagion, translation, and dissemination.[2] We refer to it as 'generative diffusion' – 'generative' because the adoption of an innovation will take different forms rather than replicate a given model, 'diffusion' because it spreads, sometimes chaotically, along multiple paths.[3]

Irrespective of the particular type of growth, the successful diffusion of an innovation depends on effective supply and effective demand: effective supply refers to the growth of evidence to show that the innovation really works. Effective demand refers to the willingness to pay. Both are needed – but sometimes the priority is to prove effectiveness while in other cases the priority is to create demand – both by persuading people that there is a need to be met, and then persuading people or organisations with the ability to pay that they should do so.[4] This is rarely easy – people usually have good reasons to resist innovations, and only adopt them if there are strong pressures (from competitors, peers, consumers, bosses), strong incentives (clear advantages over what went before), or strong emotional motivations.

Some of the methods for effective supply include investment in evaluations and research data to demonstrate effectiveness and value for money (see list of metrics below) as well as adapting models to reduce costs or improve effectiveness. The tools for effective supply include reshaping of projects to reap different kinds of economy (scale, scope, flow, penetration etc).

To grow effective demand, there may then be a need for diffusion through advocacy, raising awareness, championing a cause, and campaigning for change. Advocacy is the key to creating demand for services, particularly from public authorities – for example, making the case for public funding for drugs treatment or sex education.

As demand and supply come together, the options include the development of brands, licensing, franchising, federations as well as using some of the tools of social movements. Other important issues include the emerging fields of open licensing and open brands, as well as the evolving tools for scaling in the public sector through commissioning and procurement.

The spread of an idea also often depends on stripping out whatever is inessential. Ideas spread more easily if they are simple; modular; and don't require new skills. But complex ideas can also spread on a wide scale, though this generally takes longer, and requires more investment in professional skills.

## Inspiration

Some ideas spread because of their qualities as ideas – they are inherently inspiring, arresting, and engaging. Relatively few, however, spread on their own – more often clusters of ideas spread together, each creating the conditions for others to be received more easily.

156) **Inspiration.** Some projects spread by becoming iconic embodiments of a new way of doing things. They inspire emulation rather than replication (the approach to early years' education in Reggio Emilia for example), and need to think best about how they can respond to the enthusiasms they generate. Considering how to refine and express the idea behind the project becomes a key method for the social economy, as does developing a capacity to respond to those inspired by the idea. Projects like the BedZed housing development, or San Patrignano in Emilia Romagna, have a programme for visits and a wide range of material for others to use in order to establish their own projects.

A Pratham classroom. Pratham provides primary education to some of India's most deprived children. Images courtesy of the Pratham team.

157) **Distributed diffusion through provision as a social movement.**
Pratham in India is a good example of a simple model that has spread
on a large scale. It was originally backed by UNICEF and the city of
Mumbai, providing early years' education to children in slums. It uses
a simple model (very low cost, with no assets) and has spread by
mobilising corporate, community and philanthropic support, including
organisations in the Indian diaspora worldwide. It now operates in 21
states. It combines aspects of a social movement with effective access to
wealth and power.

## Diffusing demand

The promotion of social innovation has tended to focus on the supply side and
how innovations can be diffused among service providers through experts,
intermediaries, and collaboration. However, we argue that the design of
services should start from the user, and that its diffusion should be approached
from the perspective of users, not least because they are in many cases also co-
producers. We also argue that a distinction should be made between services
where demand can be expressed in the market (for fair trade or green goods,
for example), those where demand is expressed through the state (lobbying
for disability provisions or swimming pools, for example), and those involving
intermediate demand (public commissioning on behalf of citizens).

158) **Information for consumers.** Providing free or cheap information can
also be a means of affecting consumer behaviour and demand. This is
the case with smoking for example, or food labelling, or cheap energy
auditing.

159) **User groups and their campaigns.** User/consumer/citizen groups
play a critical role as innovators and diffusers. In health for example, the
speed of adoption of new drugs can often be correlated with the strength
of patient groups. User groups create a demand for services, particularly
from public authorities by spreading information and lobbying, . By
highlighting bad practice, and showcasing alternatives they put pressure
on businesses and the public sector to improve their products, services,
and processes. As social movements, they constitute an important
generator and diffuser of social innovation.

A Critical Mass protest in Italy. Here the protesters – who campaign for the rights of cyclists – have closed down one side of a motorway. Image courtesy of Erik Ekedahl. www.worldon2wheels.com

160) **Promotion and marketing of innovative services and programmes** to encourage behavioural change. This includes market research, market segmentation, and targeted campaigns. Examples are the '5 a day' campaign, the promotion of free smoking cessation services, and the new NHS campaign 'Change4Life' which promotes healthy activities such as playing football, practising yoga, and swimming.

161) **Brands and marks.** One way in which social markets have expanded is through the use of branding and kite marks, that both raise an awareness of the issues embodied in the offer, and provide a guarantee of the quality and good faith of the good or service. Examples include the 'Organic' and 'Fairtrade' labels.

162) **Financial or other inducements** for example, prize draws for recyclers in Canberra, or 'Healthy Incentives', the scheme being promoted by the Birmingham East and North Primary Care Trust. The incentives are given as a reward for undertaking healthy activities

agreed with their physicians. They range from mobile phone credits and childcare vouchers to health club admissions and sports tickets.

163) **Social targets.** The Chicagoland Chamber of Commerce contest, for example, looked for innovative solutions to increasing transit useage to one billion rides a year in the region; or the 10:10 project which hopes to reduce carbon emissions in the UK by 10 per cent by 2010. The 10:10 project crosses a number of sectors – involving business, government, schools, and organisations across the UK. These kinds of social targets all aim to affect public behaviour and promote a different kind of demand or activity. They encourage innovation in how to meet the target.

## Scaling and diffusion in the public sector

Scaling in the public sector has some overlaps with other fields but also important differences. Governments can grow an idea simply by legislating it, or turning it into a programme. Or they can encourage it by persuasion, or through the influence of regulators. The methods described above for sustaining an idea are also key to spreading it, including defining the idea in policy or programmes.

164) **Distributed diffusion through public policy.** New Zealand's SKIP programme (Strategies with Kids / Information for Parents) is an example of public policy working to create a scaled programme in collaboration with existing NGOs – augmenting, complementing and supplementing them within a framework that had clear outcome targets, a single brand, and common materials. Evaluations showed that it achieved considerable success with relatively little money, and explained its success as deriving from the way it helped the NGOs to work together, drew on their intelligence to design the programme, and promoted fast learning.

165) **Endorsement by regulators** for example, the impact of NICE in increasing the pressure on healthcare commissioners to take up more cost effective methods, such as smoking cessation. Through its regulatory and other powers, government can set performance and other criteria, set standards and create a 'critical' mass for the acceptance of new, or alternative, technologies and services. This removes an element of risk and encourages organisations to invest in specific technologies. It is an approach that was crucial in the emergence of the internet, GSM

Green Homes insulating a house before it is put on the market. Home Information Packs (HIPs) are now compulsory for almost all homes on the market in England and Wales. They contain a set of documents with key information relating to the property (such as property searches, proof of ownership, sustainability information, an Energy Performance Certificate (EPC) or Predicted Energy Assessment (PEA)). One of the aims of the HIP is to improve the sustainability of existing housing stock in England and Wales. Image courtesy of Bethany Murray.

and catalytic converters.

166) **Creating intermediate demand** via the professions for innovative goods and services. This could include purchasing and reusing goods made from recycled or green materials – for example, re-skinned office equipment, or 'environmentally friendly' building materials.

167) **Dissemination of best practice** through schemes such as the Beacon Awards in the UK, given to Local Authorities who excel in particular service areas. These Local Authorities then pass on best practice

through a series of events and learning visits.

168) **Global diffusion and encouragement,** for example through GBUPA, the World Bank's Global Programme on Output-Based Aid, which simultaneously encourages adoption of proven models, and ensures that aid support uses them.

169) **Change through standards** to encourage the diffusion of innovations. Examples include building regulations to increase energy efficiency, the use of sustainable materials in construction, and labelling and rating systems to support green public purchasing. Both are important in spreading innovations. For example, if the government required all new schools to be carbon-neutral, the scale of the subsequent procurement would immediately stimulate firms to develop and supply 'environmentally friendly' construction techniques. Other examples include 'smart' energy meters, Home Information Packs, or making mortgages conditional on reaching certain energy standards.

## Commissioning and procurement

Governments are big customers of goods and services – for example, the UK Government purchases £125 billion worth of goods and services per year. Alongside initiation, escalation and embedding, public procurement plays a role in relation to consolidation by purchasing services at scale.[5]

170) **Commissioning innovative services.** Commissioning has become increasingly important in the public sector, with the increase in contracting out services. Although often driven by costs, it has also been used as a means to introduce service innovation in publicly funded provision. Local government in the UK has used commissioning to experiment with alternative service models provided by social enterprises and grant based organisations, often working closely with them on extending the new practices. Another example is the NHS commissioning the health information specialists Dr Foster Intelligence to develop its information systems.

171) **Outcomes based commissioning** is where a commissioning body agrees to fund a provider on the basis that they will achieve particular agreed outcomes (rather than deliver particular outputs). The provider does not have to specify how they will achieve these outcomes. The aim is to enable providers to innovate and to create better services which

5

are tailored to the needs of service users. In the UK, this has prompted a series of developments including Local Area Agreements (LAAs) and Comprehensive Area Assessments (CAAs), which seek to base local service commissioning, delivery and evaluation on an agreed set of outcomes for that area, rather than on central targets.

172) **Developing new markets.** Government is well positioned to serve as an 'early user' of new goods and services, demonstrating their value to the wider market. The government can provide revenue and feedback which can help organisations refine their products and services so that they can compete more effectively in the global marketplace. Often this may involve purchasing more costly options in order to accelerate cost reductions.

173) **Contestability** and multiple providers to promote diversity of innovation: the aim is to design market structures in public services which create incentives for innovation. It has been one of the driving ideas behind the introduction of choice in the NHS, and of performance tables and independent assessments of schools.

174) **Practice-based commissioning** devolves commissioning powers to front line healthcare practitioners. It is based on the idea that these professionals are the best placed to make decisions regarding the needs of their patients. Practitioners are given 'virtual' budgets with which to 'buy' health services for their population, with Primary Care Trusts (PCTs) continuing to hold the 'real' budget. The main objectives are: to encourage clinical engagement in service redesign and development to bring about better, more convenient, services for patients to enable better use of resources.

175) **Payment by results** in the NHS involves paying providers a fixed price (a tariff) for each particular case treated. The national tariff is based on national average prices for hospital procedures. The system is intended to ensure a fair, consistent and transparent basis for hospital funding. It also means that funds follow patient needs and in this way is intended to support innovations and improvements in patient care.

176) **Exploratory service contracts** to ensure overt funding of innovation discovery, such as the Blue Skies Research Programmes in the UK, South Africa and New Zealand.

177) **E-procurement** involves undertaking procurement processes online. This enables commissioners to reach a wider range of potential providers and can also lead to economies in processing tenders. The public sector's procurement portal in the UK is Buying Solutions, set up in 2001.

178) **E-auctions.** Online auctions can help to achieve the greatest value for money for a given tender. The commissioning agency prepares a clear specification, and trains suppliers in the use of the software of the bidding process. The auction takes from two hours to a few days, with the bidders remaining anonymous and able to make as many bids as they wish.

179) **Framework contracts** are a means by which potential providers are 'checked over once' by an organisation, and if they meet required standards, they are then regarded as 'preferred suppliers', simplifying and speeding up purchasing. Such a contract has been used by 14 councils in the East Midlands to procure temporary agency staff over a three year period, resulting in annual cost savings of 10 per cent.

180) **Commitments from commissioners.** The commitment of a public body with the ability to purchase, commission or fund an innovation, creates the conditions for an innovation to embed and grow. One example is the advance market commitment for vaccinations if and when they are developed, which creates an incentive for R&D to be undertaken.

181) **Joint commissioning** is where two or more commissioning agents act together to co-ordinate their commissioning – taking joint responsibility for particular actions and outcomes. Joint commissioning is particularly important where there are complex needs and multiple services involved. Examples include: drug action teams; behaviour and education support teams; child and adolescent mental health services; or youth offending teams.

182) **'Share in savings' contracts,** as pioneered by the US Information Technology Management Reform Act of 1996. The Act included provisions for two pilot programmes (including one on share in savings) to test alternative contracting approaches. Share in savings is based on an agreement where the contractor pays the initial cost of implementing a new information technology system and is then paid from the savings

generated by the new system. This requires accurate measures of base line costs so that the savings can be determined.

183) **Personalised budgets** involve users being allocated a budget to be used for ongoing care needs. They are based on the idea that individuals will be able to develop their own packages of relevant support, often involving things like paying a friend to take them out which would not be part of a standard council service. The term covers self-directed support where the budget is held and spent by the individual user, and personal budgets which councils administer according to the individual's wishes. One of the best examples is In Control, a UK based charity which helps local authorities establish systems that give users this type of financial autonomy over their own care. Currently, 70,000 people in the UK receive direct payments, and another 14,000 have personal budgets. 80 per cent of public care authorities are now members of In Control (see also method 352).

## Suppliers of innovation

In particular, we will look at how the organisational structure can remain open and innovative, and reduce the overhead costs of centralised production.

184) **Developing organisational capacity** to secure the time and resources to help diffuse an innovation. This might include the ability to incubate and spin off innovations from within the organisation. One innovative approach to spinning out is the Bunsha method – when a company gets too big it is split up. Here, the company director picks a director for the new company from within the existing organisation. This new director is given enough start-up capital and decides what he/she needs in terms of staff and equipment. The parent company supports the new company until it is financially sustainable – only then can the old and new companies compete against each other. The hope is that eventually, the new company will grow until it too divides itself up creating another new firm.

185) **Growth through people.** Growth through people can take numerous forms: engaging supporters to diffuse an idea or innovation beyond organisational boundaries; spinning-out organisations to grow a field or sector; or growing an organisation's innovative capacity by investing in the professional development of staff. There is a central role for academies, apprenticeships, and training programmes. One example

Organic farming students at Everdale. Everdale is an organic farm and environmental learning centre. Its purpose is to teach sustainable living practices, and operate a model organic farm. Image courtesy of Everdale.

is Everdale in Ontario, Canada, a farm established to provide the next generation of organic farmers.

186) **Mobilising existing organisational capacity.** An alternative option is to seek out existing organisations to take up an innovation. This can be done through surveys and exploration to discover where there are capacities in existing organisations which can be mobilised to spread an innovation. The Royal National Institute for the Blind (RNIB) is a good example. The RNIB is now the sector leader for Vision 2020 UK, and through collaboration with other organizations managed to substantially grow their influence by getting all members to sign up to the agenda to improve the eye health of the UK, prevent sight loss, and improve care for those with partial or total vision loss. The collaborations between RNIB and other organizations are numerous, including television, media and book partnerships that have increased the library holdings for the blind, offered audio description in cinemas, and provided live audio description services at sporting events.[6] This is an instance where the goals of the organisation – to generally improve the quality of life for the blind – necessitated a collaborative approach to growth that has changed the organisational field, and encouraged innovation in technologies, rules, and practices.

187) **Support structures.** Different kinds of support to develop transfer packages and adaptation and learning processes are required for the generative diffusion of innovation. The NHS 'Adapt and Adopt' programme is an example which encouraged parts of the health service to take up innovations from elsewhere, but also where necessary to adapt them to different circumstances.

188) **Securing adequate supply chains for expanded production.** One of the issues in scaling is how to ensure adequate supplies of key inputs that can keep pace with developments higher up the chain. Securing a better balance between the supply capacity of fair trade producers with demand has been one of the current issues being tackled by the Fairtrade Labelling Organisation (FLO). Sales of organic food have been held back in some areas by a lack of local supply. In some social sectors the shortage is of trained people. A venture may take it on itself to ensure this synchronisation of growth, but it is also undertaken by an industry body like the Soil Association or the UK's energy efficiency body National Energy Services (NES).

189) **Adapting models** to reduce costs or improve effectiveness. A good example is the work of ASA (the Association for Social Advancement, or Asa meaning hope in Bengali) to develop an alternative to Grameen in microcredit in Bangladesh. ASA developed a very detailed guide for branch managers, focused on cost minimisation, simple paperwork, simple offices, and avoiding the requirement for groups of borrowers to guarantee the loans made to each member.

190) **Open brands.** In developing a venture's brand there are two models. There are closed brands which are tightly controlled from the centre, and which in turn require control of supply chains and all aspects of the operation that relate to the brand. This contrast with open brands, exemplified in social movements, which invite others to play a part in developing the venture and the way it connects, and is held together by a common core of meaning.

## Transmitters

We look at platforms as the nodes of the new economy, and at other ways in which users and originators can engage in the evaluation and adaption of innovation.

191) **Platforms** give people the tools and resources they need to organise themselves. They allow large groups to engage in taking up and spreading new ideas, for example via a website such as netsquared.org. People can take part as collaborators, co-producers, consumers, activists, and/or funders in new projects.

192) **Diffusion through events.** Cinepop in Mexico uses free, publicly shown movies to bring people together, and allow government bodies or local entrepreneurs that are socially driven to advertise and promote their services – ranging from microcredit to housing and sanitation.

193) **Trade fairs** are an important means of spreading information about new products, services, and organisations. They also fulfil an important networking function. They can be used as an explicit tool to spread social innovation – for example in fields such as eco-building.

194) **Diffusion through media.** For example 'Jamie's School Dinners' in the UK, which promoted healthy eating in primary and secondary schools, and led to the creation of a Trust to put its ideas into practice.

In March 2007, The University of Cambridge Programme for Sustainability Leadership and The Climate Project designed and organised a training programme at which former US Vice President Al Gore worked with 200 of the UK's top leaders from business, government, media, education and civil society. The programme brought together leaders who were committed to communicating and taking action on climate change across the UK and internationally. Image courtesy of The Climate Project.

Another interesting example is The Climate Project set up by Al Gore. This example shows that media needs to be part of a broader strategy. Gore delivered his slide show across the US (the slide show was also the basis of the film) but realised that in order to get his message across more widely, he needed to enlist supporters. He set up a programme to train people in delivering the slide show and asked that they commit to delivering it at least ten times over the following year. Gore now has a network of roughly 2,500 presenters across the US, India, Australia, Canada, and Spain. Together, these presenters have reached a worldwide audience of four million people. The presenters are kept up to date with the latest scientific findings on climate change through The Climate Project network, which also provides the volunteers with the latest version of the slide show. In 2007, Gore won the Nobel Peace

Prize in conjunction with the United Nation's Intergovernmental Panel on Climate Change (IPCC) for 'their efforts to build up and disseminate greater knowledge about man-made climate change, and to lay the foundations for the measures that are needed to counteract such change'.

195) **Associations and quasi-professional bodies** with conferences and other means of circulating information.

196) **Growth through intermediaries.** Intermediaries play a key role in the spread and diffusion of innovations by bringing together people with ideas and those with resources. In the UK, for example, the Improvement and Development Agency (IDeA) plays a critical role in local government. It works with councils in developing good practice through a network of online communities, web related resources and peer review. Another example is Australian Social Innovation Exchange (ASIX) in Australia. It is currently working on training 'embedded intermediaries' that will act as a permanent means of brokerage across the sectors thus ensuring knowledge transfer and diffusion (see also method 292).

197) **Diffusion through the web.** Viral marketing techniques can be used to tap into existing social networks and spread social ideas. SwarmTribes, an ongoing NESTA project, applies the principles of viral marketing to create a new kind of community engagement platform. The project is based on the communication principles of various social groups found in nature – such as ants, bees, geese, and dolphins.

198) **Handbooks and how to do it guides** can also be an effective means of diffusing innovative or best practice. Variations will include toolkits, oral histories, databases, and manuals. One new initiative by Open Business is the creation of a database of open business models.

199) **Barefoot consultants.** There is an important role for consultants and those with specialist knowledge – who can act as knowledge brokers and advisers in the new systems. It is best if they seek to diffuse information, acting as educators, rather than protecting their knowledge through intellectual property and charging for access.

More than 460 Barefoot Solar Engineers trained by the Barefoot College of Tilonia, Rajasthan, India have solar electrified homes in rural communities in 18 countries benefiting the rural poor who make less than $1 a day. Image courtesy of Barefoot College.

## Organisation and scale

There are currently pressures to promote mergers and takeovers within the grant economy. However, we suggest that in a distributed economy a different conception of scale is needed, one that focuses on economies of information and communication, and structures that can deliver that. Organisations within the social economy have less compulsion to organisational growth and more towards collaborative networking as a means of sharing innovation.

200) **Organisational growth** is the simplest way to grow an innovation. However it is surprisingly rare – innovations more often grow through other means. Small social enterprises and other NGOs generally find organisational growth difficult: it requires changes to leadership, culture, and structures of accountability which may not be wanted, or may be impossible.

201) **Growth through collaboration.** Collaborations are often used to develop and identify new solutions to problems through increased effectiveness, expertise, knowledge transfer, and learning. Collaboration can help institutions work better and grow – both in terms of size and impact – by increasing capacity, reducing risk, or by facilitating adaptation to changing markets and environments. Complex, multi-dimensional needs are a key site for potential collaboration. Communities of Practice are one important type of collaboration (see method 304).

202) **Small units in large systems.** Distributed organisations, namely those with many small nodes at the periphery, are well placed to diffuse innovations economically, while retaining the advantages of small and medium social enterprises, such as flexibility, drive, and dynamism.

203) **The consortium model.** In Italy, small and medium firms have developed consortia to provide collective services where scale is important. Many of these consortia are for marketing, with groups of firms having sales representatives overseas, or providing fashion and market intelligence. The cheese makers of Parma have their own brand (Parmesan) with strict rules for the production of milk and processing of the cheese. Other consortia are for technological upgrading, with consortia staff funded to scan the world technology markets, attend trade fairs and conferences, and report back to consortia members. Training, accounting, finance, and political representation are all provided through consortia, whose chief characteristic is that they are controlled by the members. They are equivalent to inter-firm co-operatives.

204) **Federations** have often been the most successful way of spreading new ideas in the social field. These depend on finding enthusiasts in many areas and then giving them considerable autonomy. This has been the model for many domestic initiatives (such as Age Concern or Emmaus), as well as international organisations such as Greenpeace or Medecins Sans Frontières. Federations often carry tensions within them (particularly when one part believes that another one is acting against underlying values); but they generally prove resilient and adaptive to change.

205) **Licensing** involves turning an innovation into intellectual property (IP) that can be protected and then licensed for use by others. Experience

of licensing in the social sector is mixed; it is often dependent on endorsement by a purchasing organisation, since IP is rarely easy to protect in the courts. It is also worth noting that the pricing of information or a service immediately reduces its spread. Greater social impact will be achieved by spreading, not restricting access to a service or information.

206) **Social franchising** is one approach to growing an organisation. It brings a number of benefits such as distribution of risk and financing. But it can only work if operations can be codified under enforceable rules. Without codification, it is difficult to ensure quality and continuity as the organisation expands. One of the main tensions is between the need on the one hand, for codification from the centre, and on the other, the need for flexibility at the periphery which is often necessary

This is Sheenagh Day, the founder of Maison Bengal and an alumnus of the School for Social Entrepreneurs, showing members of a co-operative in Kadambari in Barisal, Southern Bangladesh, a British catalogue displaying the many products produced by their co-operative. Maison Bengal is a fair trade company that works with artisan co-operatives and NGOs in Bangladesh. Image courtesy of Sheenagh Day.

to meet specifically local needs.[7] One successful social franchise is the School for Social Entrepreneurs (SSE) which uses an 'action learning' model in which participants in small groups study their own actions and experience in order to learn and improve their capacities. The original school is based in London. There are now a further seven schools in the network – Fife, Aston, East Midlands, Cornwall, Ireland, Liverpool, and Sydney, Australia. Each school is run by an independent organisation which is responsible (with support from the centre) for its own financial sustainability and programme delivery. They pay the SSE a flat annual fee of £10,000 (plus VAT) for the entire franchise package, and a licence agreement is signed with each. The package includes a 'Best Practice Guide' made up of Quality Standards and Learning Resources. Members of the Network are also supported with branding, web and technical support, policy work, media and PR, and internal/external evaluations. While the franchisees are responsible for fundraising, they get considerable support from the centre. Funding comes from a range of sources including local, regional, national government, charitable trusts, philanthropists, and commercial sponsors. Whilst participants are asked to contribute towards the cost of the programme, most places are subsidised to ensure diversity amongst participants. To date, over 360 SSE Fellows have completed programmes across the country.

207) **Mergers and acquisitions.** One way that organizations grow is through the takeover of other organizations. Growing through a takeover is not just about increasing size, but the acquisition of new technologies and capacities, the diffusion of risk, and increasing efficiency and standards. A recent example is Age UK, resulting from the merger of Age Concern England and Help the Aged in April 2009.

## Metrics to show what works and what deserves to be grown

There are many metrics for judging whether innovations are working – at various stages of development. Metrics can play a decisive role in determining whether innovations are scaled up, or deserve to be. Over several decades a great deal of work has gone into the design of measures of social value. A recent survey found 150 different metrics in use in the non-profit sector. However, relatively few of these are actually used to make decisions.

One reason why this field has failed to make progress is that there is often confusion between three different tasks performed by metrics: to provide funders or investors with data on impact; and to provide a tool for organisations to manage their own choices internally; to better understand long-term processes of social change and impact. Although these purposes overlap, any one metric cannot do all three of these tasks simultaneously, and there are direct conflicts of interest between the players involved in each of these. Here we list a few of the methods currently in use – most of which fall into the first category – or provide a means for providers of money to judge between alternatives.

208) **Standard investment appraisal methods** – there are a wide range of tools in use in banking, venture capital and other fields of investment which assess current and future cash flows, asset values, etc.

209) **Cost-benefit analysis (and its variant cost-effectiveness analysis)** has been the most widely used method, primarily by public authorities and agencies, to assess a particular proposal or project taking into account costs and benefits not reflected in market prices. An early example was undertaken in Holland to help the government decide how high to build its Polder dams. It had to take into account the cost of raising the dam by an extra metre, the value of that money in alternative uses, the likelihood of the sea rising to a certain level, and the cost in terms of human life and lost output of the sea breaching the dam and flooding the land. As a method its goal is to quantify financially what is external to the market, and is now used as standard for assessing transport investment and large development projects.

210) **Stated preference methods** monetise social value by drawing on what people say they would pay for a service or outcome. These also try to estimate what non-users might value, whether through 'altruistic use' (knowing someone else might like it); 'option use' (having the opportunity to do something); 'bequest use (leaving something for the future); and 'existence use' (satisfaction that things exist even if you don't enjoy them personally).

211) **Revealed preference methods** come from the field of economics and focus on the choices people have made in related fields in order to estimate value. 'Travel cost method' is one example, which looks at the time and travel cost expenses that people incur to visit a site as a proxy for their valuation of that site. Because travel and time costs increase with distance it's possible to construct a 'marginal willingness to pay' curve for a particular site.

212) **Social accounting matrices** and satellite accounts are used to supplement GDP with additional measures of activity and value. The OECD's Beyond GDP programme is focused on taking these forward, for example adjusting GDP figures to the greater costs associated with smaller household size.

213) Measurements of **QALYs** and **DALYs** (Quality- and Disability-Adjusted Life Years) have become a common measure for judging the cost-effectiveness of health policies and clinical interventions.

214) **Patient-Reported Outcome Measurements (PROMs)** and EQ-5D are other measures of valuing health status and patient experience. EQ-5D is a self-rating tool for patients to assess their own health status at any given point in time and can be converted into QALYs to demonstrate cost-effectiveness in relation to stated health preferences.

215) **Value-added measures** in education assess how much individual schools 'add' to the quality of pupils they take in – some schools might achieve very good exam results simply because of the quality of their intake.

216) **Social impact assessment** methods have been in use since the 1960s, trying to capture all the dimensions of value that are produced by a new policy or programme. These attempt to estimate the direct costs of an action (for example, a drug treatment programme), the probability of it working, and the likely impact on future crime rates, hospital admissions, or welfare payments. Alongside SROI (see below) and CEA, these methods include the Acumen Fund's Best Available Charitable Option (BACO) Ratio methodology (which is meant to quantify a potential investment's social output), methods developed by the Center for High Impact Philanthropy (CHIP) and various other individual foundations, all of which try to make estimates of impact by assessing probabilities, returns, and costs.

217) **Social Return on Investment** (first developed by REDF), has become increasingly popular within the non-profit world. This approach applies methods from the social impact tradition but using the language of rates of return. The benefit of SROI is helping stakeholders to recognise all of the potential benefits a project or program might have, including wider economic benefit and social returns. There are many variants in use around the world. The European Union's EQUAL Programme strongly encouraged use of measures to assess social and economic outcomes. For example, as

part of EQUAL, Finland developed an 'SYTA method' for assessing social enterprise activities. However, REDF and others have retreated from the original claim that SROI could create single number measures, describing them instead as processes for discussion between stakeholders.

218) **Social accounting methods** have been used by many countries. France's Bilan Sociétal (literally – social balance sheet) is a set of 100 indicators (ranging up to 400) showing how enterprises affect society. Italy has a similar *bilancio sociale.*

219) **Blended value methods** (associated with Jed Emerson) try to combine social and economic returns in ways that make sense to prospective investors and philanthropists.[8]

220) **Measuring public value** (particularly associated with Mark Moore), explores the value associated with public policy.[9] Some of these tie value to notions of opportunity cost (that is, what people would give up in order to receive a service or outcome whether through payments, taxes or charges); granting coercive powers to the state (for example, in return for security); disclosing private information (in return for more personalised services); giving time (for example, as a school governor); or giving up other personal resources (for example, giving blood). The BBC in the UK uses this method as an aid in decision making.

221) **Life satisfaction measures** are a particularly interesting new set of approaches (led by Professor Paul Dolan) which compare public policy and social actions by estimating the extra income people would need to achieve an equivalent gain in life satisfaction. One imaginative study of a regeneration scheme, for example, showed that modest investments in home safety – which cost about 3 per cent as much as home repairs – generated four times as much value in terms of life satisfaction.

222) **Methods within the built environment.** A Young Foundation study identified nearly 30 methods in use: some designed to guide investors, (including income capitalization methods); methods focused on profits, residuals, and replacement costs; methods using multiple regressions and stepwise regressions; methods using artificial neural networks and 'hedonic' price models (which attempt to define the various characteristics of a product or service), spatial analysis methods, fuzzy logic methods; 'auto-regressive integrated moving averages methods'; and 'triple bottom line property appraisal methods'.[10]

223) **Operational metrics,** such as those for statistical production control to spot emergent problems as prompts for innovation (see method 18). For example, a study of the operational data of public housing repairs found that the time taken to do repairs varied from a few minutes to 85 days, and the variations were getting worse. This led to a redesign of the system that lowered the average completion time to eight days and reduced the degree of variation.[11]

224) **Comparative metrics,** including cost and performance metrics/ benchmarking for operations and self-monitoring (such as those used in the New York Police Department), as well as qualitative means of evaluation and comparisons (such as awards, audits, peer assessment, or competitions such as the Singapore Public Service Awards). Another example of this is school inspections – inspectors assess and then share good practice. Comparative metrics are increasingly used by international bodies to identify policies which succeed against the grain.

225) **Balanced scorecards** are a performance measurement tool for assessing whether operational activities are aligned with broader strategic objectives.

226) **User-oriented and user-generated metrics** such as the 'sousveys' – surveys undertaken by citizens on services provided by the state – used to gather chronic disease data in Sheffield and metrics geared to self-monitoring such as those used by Active Mobs in Kent.

227) **User Experience Surveys** such as those now being introduced in the NHS which explore users' experience and emotions in relation to the service, as well as assessing health outcomes. This approach reflects the development of biographical methods as qualitative research techniques in the social sciences.

228) **Outcome benchmarks,** such as the local surveys now undertaken to measure answers to questions such as how well people get on with each other in a neighbourhood, or whether people feel a sense of influence over decisions. These generally provide a much more objective measure of social dynamics than the indicators chosen by individual organisations to prove their impact.

229) **Assessment as learning,** including peer reviews and real time evaluation methods to promote cross-pollination such as NESTA's evaluation of Health Launchpad.

**End notes**

1. See for example, Dees, G., Battle Anderson, B. and Wei-Skillern, J. (2004) Scaling Social Impact: Strategies for Spreading Social Innovations. 'Stanford Social Innovation Review.' Spring; Bradach, J. (2003) Going to Scale: the challenge of replicating social programs. 'Stanford Social Innovation Review.' Spring; McLeod Grant, H. and Crutchfield, L.R. (2007) Creating High Impact Non Profits. 'Stanford Social Innovation Review.' Fall.

2. A good summary of diffusion studies can be found in Åberg, P. (2008) 'Translating Popular Education: Civil Society Cooperation between Sweden and Estonia.' Stockholm: Stockholm University. Chapter 5; see also Strang, D. and Soule, S.A. (1998) Diffusion in Organizations and Social Movements: From Hybrid Corn to Poison Pills. 'Annual Review of Sociology.' 24, pp.265-290; and Oliver, P.E. and Myers, D. (1998) 'Diffusion Models of Cycles of Protest as a Theory of Social Movements.' Congress of the International Sociological Association, Montreal. July, 1998.

3. For more information on growing innovations, see Rogers, E.M. (2003) 'Diffusion of innovations.' New York: Free Press.

4. Mulgan, G., Ali, R., Halkett, R. and Sanders, B. (2007) 'In and Out of Sync: The challenge of growing social innovations.' London: NESTA.

5. The 'initiation, escalation and consolidation' model is discussed in: Edler J. *et al.* (2005) 'Innovation and Public Procurement. Review of Issues at Stake'. Study for the European Commission, Final Report. Fraunhofer Institute for Systems and Innovation Research. Available at: ftp://ftp.cordis.europa.eu/pub/innovation-policy/studies/full_study.pdf. For more information on procurement and commissioning see: Stoneman, P. and Diederen, P. (1994) Technology Diffusion and Public Policy. 'The Economic Journal.' 104 (July), pp.918-930. Oxford: Blackwell; Georghiou, L. (2007) 'Demanding Innovation: Lead Markets, Public Procurement and Innovation.' Provocation. London: NESTA; Office of Government Commerce (2004) 'Capturing Innovation: nurturing suppliers' ideas in the public sector.' London: Office of Government Commerce; CBI/QinetiQ (2006) 'Innovation and Public Procurement: A new approach to stimulating innovation.' London: CBI; HM Treasury (2007) 'Transforming Government Procurement.' London: HM Treasury.

6. RNIB (2008) 'Transforming Lives: Annual Review 2007/08.' London: RNIB.

7. See Ahlert, D. *et al.* (2008) 'Social Franchising: a way of systematic replication to increase social impact.' Berlin: Association of German Foundations; Tracey, P. and Jarvis, O. (2006) An Enterprising Failure: Why a promising social franchise collapsed. 'Stanford Social Innovation Review.' Spring, pp.66-70, 2006; and Yamada, K. (2003) One Scoop, Two Bottom Lines: Nonprofits are buying Ben & Jerry's franchises to help train at-risk youth. 'Stanford Social Innovation Review.' Summer, 2003.

8. Emerson, J. (2003) 'The Blended Value Map: Tracking the intersects and opportunities of economic, social and environmental value creation.' Available at: http://www.blendedvalue.org/

9. Moore, M.H. (1995) 'Creating Public Value: Strategic Management in Government.' Cambridge, MA: Harvard University Press.

10. Mulgan, G. *et al.* (2006) 'Mapping Value in the Built Urban Environment.' A Report to the Commission for Architecture and the Built Environment. London: CABE.

11. This example is discussed in Seddon, J. (2003) Freedom from Command and Control. 'Vanguard Education.' Chapter 5. Seddon discusses the principles of operational metrics based on flow.

# 6 SYSTEMIC CHANGE

The most transformative innovations have been the ones that combine many elements in a new way. The car, for example, can be thought of as a combination of many innovations – combustion engines, tyres, electrical systems, road traffic management, and driving schools. The mobile phone combines microprocessors, transmitters, networks of masts, payment models, and so on. The welfare state combines legal rights, service delivery systems, assessment tools, and tax collection models.

In this section we look at more fundamental innovations that are systemic in nature. By this we mean innovations that radically transform some of the fundamental systems on which we depend – how food is provided, healthcare, housing, or learning – according to fundamentally different principles. These invariably involve many different elements.

Systemic innovation is very different from innovation in products or services. It involves changes to concepts and mindsets as well as to economic flows: systems only change when people think and see in new ways. It involves changes to power, replacing prior power holders with new ones. And it usually involves all four sectors – business, government, civil society, and the household.

Models for thinking about innovation that only look at one sector miss the crucial ways in which they interact. For example: innovation around carbon reduction has been driven by the green movement over many decades; reinforced by politicians introducing new laws and regulations; and then amplified by businesses and clean technology investment funds. It has involved new technologies, but these have been enablers rather than sufficient conditions for change. Often it's been more important to develop new ways of organising transport, housing, or energy, or new ways for citizens to think about their own responsibilities. For some of the same reasons systemic innovation is by its nature highly social – usually involving many leaders, many allies, and battles on many fronts.

Systemic innovations can be suddenly pushed forward by a crisis or a disruptive technology. More often, they are the result of slow but cumulative processes entailing changing infrastructures, behaviours, and cultures. Examples include the creation of welfare states after the Second World War, the spread of comprehensive early years' education programmes in Europe, dramatic expansions of higher education, and the spread of democracy.

A good example is the transformation of how household waste is handled – from landfill and incineration as a predominant approach to greater use of composting, anaerobic digestion, and recycling. This has required new laws, regulations, business models, habits in the home (separating waste), collection systems, and new ways of reusing and recycling materials. Systemic innovation in local areas has brought the transformation of transport (for example in Curitiba) and of housing (for example in Vauban, Germany) and public healthcare (for example in Karelia, Finland). The web has also brought systemic innovation to retailing and news, and has the potential (albeit not yet realised) to achieve fundamental change in healthcare and education.

The very complexity of systemic innovation makes it hard to define specific tools which can advance it. Every system has some unique properties, and unique power structures. But there are some common elements, and looking back through history it is clear that strategies for systemic innovation usually include:

- The formation of progressive coalitions that bring together different partners.

- Intensive processes to build up shared diagnoses and visions.

- Efforts to grow a critical mass of practical examples.

- New rights.

- Training a group of professionals and practitioners with both new skills and attitudes.

- Pre-empting inflexible conventional technologies that freeze disruptive forms of innovation.

- Accessing professional and other expertise for the contest of evidence.

- Implementing legal and regulatory devices to embed change.

- Empowering the beneficiaries of the new system.

In stable times, systemic innovation is rare – primarily because there are insufficient incentives for change. Incumbents tend to deflect threats, or to reinterpret radical new ideas in ways that fit existing power structures. The challenge of climate change, for example, is reinterpreted as simply a new set of taxes and regulations, or a new set of investment devices.

Systematic approaches to innovation are rare. But the UK health service may be becoming a good case study. It is a huge system by any standards with an annual turnover of £98 billion and employing some 1.5 million staff. It is already heavily involved in innovation through investment in research and development on pharmaceuticals and medical instruments, and close links with top universities such as Imperial and UCL, as well as with big firms like GlaxoSmithKline and Pfizer. But in recent years it has recognised that these traditional tools, while useful, do not go far enough. Some of the biggest impacts on health outcomes now come from service innovations, and some of the greatest creativity comes from outside the sphere of clinical leaders, business and government. Hence the drive to link many of the tools described earlier, from grants, loans and equity to commissioning, purchasing and whole system examples. All of these aim to ease the shift from a system primarily focused around hospitals and doctors to one in which patients share responsibility for care, supported by detailed feedback systems – in which whole environments are reshaped to support healthier living.

Such top-down efforts succeed only to the extent that they mobilise the enthusiasm and commitment of thousands of practitioners. Some innovators start from the other end, and many community-driven initiatives have tried to accelerate systemic innovation – such as the Transition Towns movement, or the Slow Food movement. The great challenge for top-down programmes is how to engage the enthusiasm and commitment of the public. The great challenge for bottom-up ventures is how to access the power and money to shift big systems.

For any individual innovator there are choices to be made about where to direct energies. Should they direct their energy to policy and law, demonstration projects, advocacy, arguments, campaigns, or research? And should they work through existing organisations, new ones, coalitions, or as lone voices? Profound system change commonly includes some actions in all the different permutations which follow from these choices.

Here we show first some of the organising ideas that are generating systemic change at the moment, and then some of the methods which contribute to making change happen. There are many other examples – from new models of personal finance to new models of university. The key is that in every example systemic change involves the interaction of ideas, movements, models, and interests.

## Ideas that energise systemic innovations

We have shown how new frames and ideas can prompt innovation. These can be even more important in giving shape to systemic changes – helping the participants to make sense of their changing roles. Here we list a few of the generative paradigms that are prompting systemic innovation in some fields.

230) **Distributed production.** The idea of a radical decentralisation of formerly centralised production is recasting many services. In energy services, for example, localised energy systems are reappearing, linked both to domestic energy generation through renewables, or micro combined heat and power, and through the development of community trigeneration systems such as those in Woking and London. There are similar patterns emerging in healthcare (the home as hospital), education (online learning), and social care.

231) **Changing the 'scripts' around services.** The script of a service or practice provides its meaning and rationale. The 19th century introduced many new scripts around health and hygiene. The 20th century rewrote the scripts about income inequality and welfare. Many of the public service scripts we have inherited are now being reassessed. One example is waste disposal. In the past it has been seen as a problem of public health. Now it has been re-scripted as a resource. Instead of waste disposal being the end point of a product's linear progress from 'cradle to grave', the new script talks of a circular process of 'cradle to

cradle'. Scrap paper is returned to be reworked at paper mills. Drink cans are returned to the smelter. 'End of life' cars and electronic goods are disassembled and their components and materials reworked as part of a closed loop. Thinking, in terms of loops and zero waste, has reshaped systems for handling household and business waste, and led to new regulations, directives, business models, and public attitudes.

232) **Prevention.** Many new scripts are about investing in prevention rather than financing the costs of neglect. This has been a guiding principle in the redesign of manufacturing processes to reduce delays and cut out avoidable processes (like reworks of defective items). But it is also an over-arching principle for many public services. Zero Waste is a case in point. So is the slow re-orientation of healthcare services from illness to the creation of conditions for positive living. The modern versions of the 1930s Peckham experiment to create holistic environments for healthier living are a good example, like a number of the UK's Healthy Living Centres. They represent a return to what was the norm for most of the last two thousand years in the many literatures advocating how to live a good life. Today such an approach can draw on abundant evidence on the impact of positive health on the avoidance of disease and quick recovery.

233) **Investing early.** The benefits of investing early are not only preventative – to avoid costs later down the line – but to make future services more effective and fulfilling. An example, which could be applied in other fields, is holistic early years' education provision. These programmes rethink human potential by dealing upstream with the causes of educational success and failure. The programmes have steadily built up evidence and support over forty years, particularly in northern Europe and in the USA. Examples include the Abecedarian project and Sure Start providing intensive support for children to reduce risk factors. Where these succeed they create a political constituency for public investment in early years' education as well as effective models for delivery.

234) **New models of the support economy.** These reorient services around support for the user rather than the simple delivery of a standardised package. The idea has led to radical models for reshaping care for the elderly, for example, that involve new platforms, and combinations of professional and mutual support (such as the digital spine for communication and service delivery in rural Maine).

These are envac points at the Hammarby Sjöstad low-carbon housing development in Stockholm, Sweden. Waste is dropped in the inlets – a vacuum system sucks it to the collection terminal where it is sorted. It is a working prototype for a new and sustainable way of living. Image courtesy of Liz Bartlett.

235) **Low or zero carbon living** of the kind promoted in new eco-towns and cities such as Hammarby Sjöstad, and the Sonoma Mountain Village in Northern California, which involve radical rethinking of patterns of daily life – from work and transport to housing design and finance.

236) **Holistic support models for services** such as The Key, Ten UK's support service for head teachers which provides support for every aspect of school management.

237) **Personalized support services** such as personal health and fitness coaches, increasingly backed up by shared data services and networks. Service design in the 1980s and 1990s often focused on disaggregating services, creating back offices separate from the front line, and breaking services into modular elements. In practice this often led to lower

customer satisfaction, and greater duplication. Hence the current drive to more personalised and integrated service design

238) **Support models that mobilise citizen energy,** such as Canada's Circles of Support, and investment in community-based solutions focused on prevention. These are part of a 'family' of innovations in criminal justice that see the offender in their social context and mobilise that context to help both with punishment and rehabilitation.

239) **Systemic drives to energise and empower marginalised groups,** such as victims of trafficking, or adolescent girls. We often think of systemic change being led by the public sector. However, there are examples of non-profit organisations trying to effect change on a systemic level. The Nike Foundation's work to develop the ability of adolescent girls in developing countries to deliver social and economic change to their families and communities, is an interesting example of a foundation tackling issues of marginalisation in a systemic way (see the diagram below).

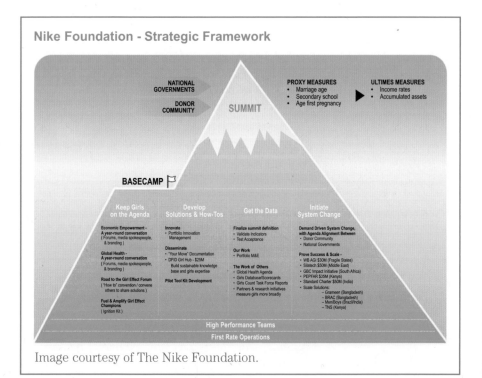

Image courtesy of The Nike Foundation.

240) **Post-chronologism.** Innovations to transform life patterns away from the 20th century focus on chronological age as the determinant of when you should work, learn and retire. This idea leads to a range of innovations in everything from employment law and pensions to volunteering and urban design.[1]

241) **Radical democratisation,** taking the principles of popular sovereignty into new spaces, from the mass media to local government and the workplace. This involves a wide range of issues from the use of the web, to the nature of technology and the design of distributed systems which provide spaces for people to contribute to projects directly, as a form of productive democracy. It also requires innovatory forms of engagement like participatory budgeting, changes in the forms of ownership, and public accounting.

242) **Trust-creating devices,** including technologically-based models to quickly judge whether someone can be trusted as a service provider or collaborator. These include the now familiar reputational devices being used on networks like eBay, and more formal legal devices (like public databases). With the increasing mixing of voluntary and professional roles (for example around care for the elderly, or education), tools of this kind are becoming ever more important.

## Infrastructures and interstructures to support new systems

Some new systems depend on infrastructures. Widespread broadband infrastructures, for example, are the precondition for some new models of care in the home; mobile phone infrastructures may be the precondition for organising new models of low-cost banking.

243) **Creating new infrastructure,** or adapting old ones, is necessary for the expansion of new systems (such as the development of smart grids, charging points for electric cars, or the pipe network for distributing heat, power and cooling).[2]

244) **Data infrastructures.** A different, and controversial, infrastructure is the creation of a single database of children deemed 'at risk' in the UK. This was seen as crucial to creating a holistic set of services to deal with children's needs, but ran into acute problems of implementation and profound fears about the implications for civil liberties.

Infrastructure for green transport - plug-in points for hybrid cars in San Francisco. Image courtesy of CalCars.org.

245) **Platform infrastructures,** such as feedback sites on public services or M-PESA's platform for phone-based banking.

246) **Rewiring economies,** connecting sectors like the utilities and automotive industries for the development of plug-in hybrid cars, or promoting new supply or processing chains, such as new or expanded industries to recover and process secondary materials.

247) **Technical innovations for key points in the chain** such as home medical testing equipment or biodegradable plastic bags, that then enable systemic innovation around them.

## Formation of users and producers

Users and citizens often need to play a part in the design and implementation of new systems. They may require new skills and approaches (what the

French term 'formation') as may professionals and managers. This is evident in many of the examples listed above – such as personalised healthcare which requires patients to become more skilled in monitoring and managing their own conditions, and healthcare professionals to expand their skills of personal support.

248) **Innovation academies** embodying new principles for training, action research, and formation. Examples include the College of Health, and Forum for the Future. Mondragon University and Centro Popular de Cultura e Desenvolvimento (Brazil) go further, giving students the experience of working in small social enterprises. These could play a critical role in training up a future cadre of social innovators.

249) **Mutual help and mentoring by users.** The tradition of voluntary coaching (in sports clubs, or the arts, for example) is being extended to education, to care of the elderly, and to those with chronic health conditions. The Expert Patients Programme (NHS/EPP) is an example of this trend, where citizens with particular medical conditions provide advice and training sessions to others with similar conditions. Systems of mutual support have been particularly well developed among people with mental illness.

250) **Engaging citizens in whole system change processes.** In Karelia, Finland, for example, citizens played a critical role in redesigning the public health system. In 1972 they launched a petition to get help to reduce the high incidence of cardiovascular disease. The result – the North Karelia Project – was a collaboration between local and national authorities, experts, and local citizens. Together they formulated and implemented a series of community-based interventions intended to prevent the incidence of cardiovascular disease. The project has had a dramatic impact, helping to reorganise the health system around prevention and healthy living, and by involving citizens in the design and implementation of the programme, served as a process for community learning. The project has acted as a major demonstration programme for national and international applications.

251) **Support for new patterns of power and responsibility,** for example – for self-care for chronic disease, that combines rich data feedback with support structures which help patients understand and treat their own conditions more effectively.

## Strategic moves that accelerate systems change

Every story of systemic innovation involves key moments when the tables are turned on older models and incumbents.

252) **Creating new evidence** and facts in the contest of evidence (for example the Schiphol airport noise campaign), or the development of new measurements of well-being to shift public policy towards holistic goals (such as the OECD programme on Beyond GDP).

253) **Establishing working prototypes of the new system,** for example the low carbon housing in Vauban in Switzerland, and Bed Zed in the UK.

254) **Designing and trialling platforms to trigger systemic innovation** including peer-to-peer models such as the School of Everything and digital learning environments such as colleges in second life.

255) **Comprehensive pilots,** such as the Bastoey Island prison in Norway – a low cost 'ecological' prison in which prisoners produce their own food, use solar energy, and maximise recycling. In healthcare, the Whole System Demonstrators initiated by the NHS in Cornwall, Kent and Newham are further examples designed to test an integrated model of health and social care, making use of new telehealth and telecare technology (see also method 89).

256) **Blocking technology** and other investment choices that will impede changes to systems. This is particularly relevant to key infrastructures with high fixed costs, as in energy or water provision. Stopping sunk investment, or reinvestment, in an old model can be the key to creating space for investment in new alternatives.

257) **Frames for change.** Framing involves linking particular events – such as natural disasters, crises of care or of the economy – to underlying causes, and using this as the basis for proposing major systemic change. Here, the combination of framing, communications techniques, and campaigning are critical: for example, using the tragedy of deaths of older people from heat waves to advance radical change in how social support is organised.

## Regulatory and fiscal changes

Almost every systemic change involves legislation and the state at some point. There are a few exceptions, such as the rise of new online infrastructures for retailing. But every movement involved in profound change, from the environment to equality, has depended on recognition of its principles in law. New legislative and regulatory architectures can be the keys to unlocking systemic change, whether through new rights or new trading or building standards, social and environmental performance requirements, or new ways of handling or measuring value.

258) **New rights** such as rights to care, rights to schooling or rights to vote. These are usually the result of a long period of campaigning, and lead to new demands on systems of provision, that often lead to service and process innovation.

259) **New responsibilities** such as responsibilities to care for children, or producer responsibility for reducing carbon emissions and environmental pollution. Another promoter and diffuser of innovation is the introduction by central government of statutory responsibility for local government to address particular issues.

260) **New forms of property,** such as establishing owner's 'use it or lose it' responsibilities for particular assets; propertising formerly free goods such as airwaves or the use of the oceans; and establishing the terms of property and access for intellectual and cultural intangibles.

261) **Legal bans.** These can be a powerful tool, though usually in conjunction with other methods. Examples include bans on smoking in workplaces in part of Europe, and on advertising billboards in São Paolo, Brazil.

262) **Enforcement.** A related point is the serious enforcement of new laws, for example on polluters, domestic violence, or forced marriages.

263) **Formal classifications** can shift systems, for example through redefining what counts as recycling and therefore eligible for particular grants/prices; or redefining chronic drug use as a health issue rather than a criminal justice issue.

264) **Targets with penalties** and various quasi-market schemes as in packaging regulations, or the UK Landfill Allowance Trading Scheme.

265) **Regulatory requirements,** for example, that all towns and villages with more than 2,000 inhabitants should have separate bio waste collection as proposed in the EU's draft Biowaste directive.

266) **Tax and fiscal structures.** Re-calibrating markets through, for example, fiscal and pricing regimes such as the German (now Europe-wide) feed-in tariffs for renewable energy. These provide access to markets (i.e. direct access to the grid), long term contracts, and minimum prices – parallel in many ways to the mechanisms of fair trade, and to contracting by paper mills for recycled paper (though in the case of feed-in tariffs the arrangement has been mandated by regulation). Reduced VAT rates have also been used in Europe to encourage environmental investment, as with home insulation in the UK, biofuels, renewable energy equipment and recycled paper in the Czech Republic, and the equipment for the production and use of renewable energy in Portugal. Such incentives are likely to be most effective when they are linked to regulation (such as the requirement to fit condensing boilers in the UK, or the phasing out of incandescent light bulbs) where they reduce the cost differential of the green alternatives.

## Information, accounting and statistics

Information and accounting systems can block innovation – in many cases, they will need to be reorganised to enable or reinforce systemic change. What gets measured shapes what gets done. In many fields, attempts are underway to reshape measurement to better handle holistic systems effects. So while familiar data on income, employment, diseases or educational achievement continues to be gathered, there is growing interest in other types of measurement that may give more insights into what needs to be done – for example, focusing on fear of crime as well as crime itself; on cultures of health behaviour as well as physical disease; and on trust in institutions as well as their formal processes.

267) **Information systems that reinforce systemic change.** For example, ways of measuring emissions in real time, or that make costs and inefficiencies transparent. In developing systems of sustainable production, Life Cycle Analysis has become a standard for assessing the energy, atmospheric and materials impact of a particular product, and provides signposts for innovation at those stages of the process, or for specific materials, which have a disproportionately negative impact.

268) **Restructured public accounting** and finance to create positive feedback loops that further systemic change, such as personal budgets in health that create constituencies for radical reorganisation. Requiring public agencies to publish data on their balance sheets, or to show disaggregated spending patterns, or flows of costs, can then contribute to momentum towards systems redesign, as can the consolidation of spending data for particular areas or groups of people. Too often, public accounting has been structured around the issues of targets, control, and incentives, rather than user-oriented operational issues. The move towards customer-driven management information systems that has transformed industrial and service processes in the market sector, would have a similar transformative impact in the public sphere.

269) **Measures of true progress.** Since 2004 the OECD has been running a programme on new measures of social progress. In 2009 it launched Wikiprogress, bringing together data and analysis on progress. The same year President Sarkozy commissioned Joseph Stiglitz to chair an inquiry into new measures of GDP. The commission recommended far-reaching changes, including paying attention to non-paid work, rethinking the contribution of finance to prosperity, and properly accounting for environmental impacts. All of these changing measures point to some radically different ways of organising public policy.

## Progressive coalitions and social movements

Social movements often act as champions of systemic alternatives, for example mobilising people with disabilities to engage in the redesign of cities, and lobbying for reforms to legislation and regulation. Progressive coalitions play a critical role in mobilising support for systemic changes.

270) **Social movements focused on lifestyle innovation and transformation,** such as the feminist and green movements but also including, for example, Transition Towns, the global network of several hundred towns seeking to move to low carbon living. In the past, war, particularly with conscripted armed forces, has been a major instigator of system change. Today this role is being played by social movements.

271) **Growing self-organising social movements.** In the green movement, for example, Camp for Climate Action is the fastest growing grass roots movement of diverse people taking action on climate change. The group organises festival-like camps, direct action, protests, swoops, and a

Climate Camp at Drax coal-fired power station in West Yorkshire. This was the first protest organised by campaigning group, Camp for Climate Change. In 2006, 600 people gathered outside the power station – the UK's biggest single source of carbon dioxide - for ten days of learning and sustainable living, which culminated in a day of mass action against the power station. The group's stated aim is to 'kick-start a social movement to tackle climate change' and in this they have proved very successful. Image courtesy of Akuppa.

series of learning events.

272) **Organising formal coalitions for change** with explicit goals, and broadly agreed roles for different sectors – for example to create a new system of apprenticeships in green industries, or to green existing industries.

## Systemic finance

We describe many different finance tools in other sections which can contribute to systemic change. For investment funds to finance truly systemic ideas they need different methods to those used for investment in established systems. At an early stage there is unlikely to be any clear revenue model, or any benchmarks to draw on. Instead, assessments need to include some judgement of the broader direction of change in the field as a whole; some judgement about the qualities of the key individuals; and some rough assessments of the relational capital they bring. Not surprisingly, these tools and approaches are rare – and require a great deal of confidence in the funding agency as well as in those receiving funds.

273) **Public finance for systems change.** The design of public finance can underpin systemic innovation. Integrating control over budgets that have previously been split between different agencies can make it much easier to innovate – for example on the boundaries between health and care, or environment and transport.

274) **The creation of new investment flows** can do the same, particularly when these are supported by new kinds of property or asset, such as the Clean Development Mechanism (CDM) in climate change. This mechanism allows a country with an Emissions Reduction Target to initiate an Emission Reduction Project in a developing country, that in turn earns a tradeable Certified Emissions Reduction (CER) credit, that can count towards the initiating country's Kyoto target.

275) **Finance for systemic prevention.** Changing funding flows can also encourage preventative services. One example is Oregon's Justice Reinvestment programme – a local approach to justice decision making which seeks to reinvest some of the state funds spent on imprisonment into local programmes that tackle the longer term causes of offending in specific localities. It diverts funds away from prisons and back towards local communities. It was first introduced to reduce the rate of reoffending among young offenders in Oregon in the late 1990s. The state handed over a 'block-grant' to Deschutes County which was equal to the amount of money the state spent each year on imprisoning young offenders from that county, thereby making the county and not the state financially responsible for young offenders in custody. The county were free to choose how to allocate the funds on the basis that they would be 'charged-back' the costs of sending the young offenders back to prison.[3] Deschutes County then implemented a series of resettlement and prevention programmes within the community which resulted in a 72 per cent fall in the number of young people being sent to prison. This model has been tested in a number of states including Ohio, Michigan,

Arizona, Vermont, Pennsylvania and Texas, where it has delivered significant results.[4]

**End notes**

1. Schuller, T. (1995) My time with MY. In: Dench, G., Gavron, K. and Flower, T. (Eds.) (1995) 'Young at Eighty.' pp.204-205.
2. Department of Energy and Climate Change (2009) 'Smarter Grids: The Opportunity, 2050 Roadmap.' Discussion Paper. London: Department of Energy and Climate Change.
3. Allen, R. and Stern, V. (Eds) (2007) 'Justice Reinvestment – A New Approach to Crime and Justice.' The International Centre for Prison Studies. London: King's College. Available at: http://www.kcl.ac.uk/depsta/law/research/icps/downloads/justice-reinvestment-2007.pdf
4. Ibid.

# SECTION 2: CONNECTING PEOPLE, IDEAS AND RESOURCES

## Intermediaries

Intermediaries are individuals, organisations, networks, or spaces which connect people, ideas, and resources. They can take a variety of forms – some incubate innovations by providing a 'safe' space for collaboration and experimentation; some connect entrepreneurs with the supports they need to grow their innovations; and others help to spread innovations by developing networks and collaborations.

A crucial lesson of innovation in other fields is that the supply of ideas, and demand for them, do not automatically link up. In the technology sector a great variety of institutions exist to connect them better. They include specialists in technology transfer, venture capital firms, conferences, and academic journals – which sit alongside consultants adept at looking at companies' IP, or their R&D pipelines, spotting patterns and possibilities that aren't visible to managers and owners themselves. Much of the history of technology has confirmed how important these 'social connectors' are. They are one of the reasons why economics has found it hard to understand innovation without a substantial dose of sociology added in.

The social field generally lacks specialist intermediaries of this kind. There are some effective networks in academic disciplines and professions. And some foundations try hard to connect emerging ideas to potential buyers and users. But these tend to be small scale and ad hoc. This is one of the reasons why it can take so long for ideas to grow and achieve impact in the social field.

As social innovation becomes more widely understood, new institutions are coming into existence to fill this gap. These range from innovation funds to innovators in residence, and innovation agencies. Building-based projects have been the fastest to take off – because their business model draws on the fact that any new venture needs to be based somewhere, and people tend to like to congregate with others like them.

In the medium term however, as in private business, we would expect social economy intermediaries to become more explicitly focused on their knowledge and relationships. One of their roles is to grow fields and markets: supporting a range of social ventures to become more effective in tackling social problems.

We've suggested that much social innovation comes from linking up the 'bees' – the individuals and small organisations that are buzzing with ideas and imagination – and the 'trees', the bigger institutions that have power and money but are usually not so good at thinking creatively. On their own, the bees can't achieve impact. On their own, the trees find it hard to adapt.

Intermediaries can help to link them up. To be effective they need to reach across the boundaries that divide sectors, disciplines, and fields. They need to attract innovative, entrepreneurial people – the job of intermediation needs to be highly creative. And they need to be fluent in many 'languages' – able to translate from the 'language of everyday needs' to the very different 'languages' of policymakers or investors, for example.

Intermediaries also play a critical role at the stages of growth and diffusion. They are often involved in designing, testing and evaluating projects, subsequently advocating their adoption by government, businesses and non-profit organisations. They help to establish markets for new services and projects, and to spread innovations by developing networks which highlight, promote and disseminate learning and best practice. These are sometimes strongly promoted by funders – for example, the European Commission's sustainable urban development network URBACT and the EQUAL Programme.

## Championing innovation

Individual roles can be created to scout out, highlight, and disseminate innovations. These individuals can work within, or across, organisations. They can be involved in adopting or adapting existing innovations. Or, they can be responsible for embedding processes within an organisation to enable innovation to flourish. These kinds of role are increasingly popular within the public sector.

276) **Innovation scouts** are responsible for discovering innovations which can be adapted, adopted, or replicated within their organisation. Small and medium firms in northern Italy, such as the clothing producers in Carpi, Emilia Romagna, form consortia to fund scouts of this kind. The scouts travel to international trade fairs and conferences to identify the latest technologies, and then report back through the region's Centres for Real Services. The Young Foundation has employed an experienced investigative journalist to play a similar role in healthcare, scanning for promising new projects, and looking in detail at which elements could be adapted or replicated.

277) **Innovation champions** are individual consultants who produce ideas, network to find what else is being tried, and build coalitions of support. They embed processes and procedures within their organisations to develop a more creative culture which encourages new ideas and experimentation. The co-operative movement has developed a number of intermediaries of this kind.

278) **Social intrapreneurs** are people who work inside large organisations to develop and promote practical solutions to social or environmental challenges. Social intrapreneurs apply the principles of social entrepreneurship inside a major organisation. They can also be characterised by an 'insider-outsider' mindset and approach.[1] One example is Win Sakdinan at Procter & Gamble who developed the company's Future Friendly initiative, which helps consumers to save energy, water and packaging with its brands.[2] Another example is the nurses as social entrepreneurs programme developed at Oxford University's Saïd Business School.

279) **Social entrepreneurs in residence** are entrepreneurs who are brought in to develop the innovative capacities of an organisation. One recent example is the Young Foundation's Social Entrepreneur in

Residence programme at Birmingham East and North Primary Care Trust (BEN PCT). The social entrepreneur in residence is tasked with shaping the environment of BEN PCT so that innovation becomes embedded and is hard-wired into its systems and processes. Acting as a catalyst to spot talent and scout for ground breaking ideas, the social entrepreneur in residence aims to develop three or more social enterprises to improve local health outcomes within the first 12 months of the project.

The Saheli Women's Centre in Balsall Heath, Birmingham. This is one of the projects being supported by the Social Entrepreneur in Residence at Birmingham East and North Primary Care Trust (BEN PCT). Dry slope skiing is one of the sports and social activities that Saheli organises for its predominantly Asian community. Image courtesy of Bill Knight / www.knightsight.co.uk

## Innovation teams

There is a wide range of innovation teams. Some work within organisations, either within or across departments, some are set up to encourage collaboration across organisations, and some are designed to focus on particular issues – or use a particular approach. The best innovation teams are multidisciplinary and able to engage a wide range of stakeholders in the design, development, and evaluation of innovation.

280) **In-house innovation units,** such as NESTA's Public Services Innovation Lab (launched in 2009) which supports a range of different social start-ups. Another example is MindLab in Denmark, set up by the Ministry of Economic and Business Affairs, the Ministry of Taxation, and the Ministry of Employment, to bring together government, private enterprises, and the research community under one roof to promote user-centred innovation.

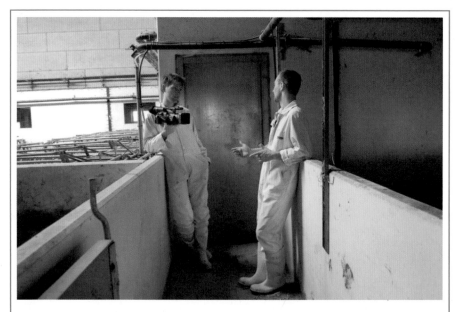

A day in the life. In order to promote user-centred innovation, MindLab undertake ethnographic research, including video diaries, to understand the everyday needs and ideas of Danish citizens better. Image courtesy of MindLab.

## Innovation structures and incentives

Traditionally, the private market has been seen as the primary source of innovation. This is because it has the structures, mechanisms, and incentives that drive innovation. In Joseph Schumpeter's formulation, it has the power of 'creative destruction', destroying the old in order to open the way for the new. Neither the state nor the grant economy has the structure or incentive to innovate in this way. It is argued that they lack the mechanisms that allow the best to flourish and the less effective to wither away (although until the late 19th century many technological innovations were associated with governments and armies rather than markets).[6] The household on the other hand – that most distributed of economic systems – generates ideas but on its own lacks the capital, surplus time, and organisational capacity to develop them.

Here, we look at some of the methods used within each sector to promote innovation, using a sectoral lens to complement the focus on stages used in Section I.

### End notes

1. Murray, R. (2009) 'Danger and Opportunity: Crisis and the new Social Economy.' Provocation. London: NESTA.
2. This is a wider definition than the more usual one which refers to the social economy as the third sector – namely NGOs and social enterprises. The definition here includes both the public economy – whose values and goals have much in common with those of the third sector – and the informal economy of the household.
3. The social components of these three sub economies outside the state are the economic parallel to civil society, and could be thought of as the civil economy, that is to say that part of the social economy that is outside the state.
4. There are also interfaces within each sub economy, for example between the private and social markets. This may take the form of joint ventures, as in the recent case of Grameen-Danone and their collaboration in a social enterprise producing yoghurt for low income households in Bangladesh.
5. Maxmin, J. and Zuboff, S. (2004) 'The Support Economy: Why Corporations are Failing Individuals and the Next Episode of Capitalism.' New York: Penguin.
6. This is the argument of Beinhocker, E. (2007) 'The Origin of Wealth.' Cambridge, MA: Harvard Business School Press. He puts forward an evolutionary model of growth, parallel to that of Darwin, in which the market is the primary mechanism of selection. The parallel between ecological and market economic mechanisms is one reason why many in the environmental movement are attracted to modified markets as the adequate economic form, but this does not deal with those areas of the economy which are difficult to commodify.

# 1 SUPPORT IN THE PUBLIC SECTOR

In the past, governments were often pioneers of social innovation. The great municipal reforms of the 19th century created a new social infrastructure, as did the welfare reforms of the late 19th and 20th centuries. More recently some of the most important technological innovations were associated with public organisations – from the Internet (DARPA) to the world wide web (CERN). But there are many structural features of government that inhibit risk taking and innovation. There are barriers (from cost based budgeting and departmental structures, to audit and accountability processes, as well as a lack of career rewards) and few enabling conditions such as the dedicated budgets, teams, and processes found in business or science. These conditions too often squeeze out new ideas and impose standardised solutions rather than allowing many flowers to bloom.

The result is not necessarily a lack of innovation in government.[1] Government at every level has been the site of almost constant change – particularly in the last 30 years. The problem is that the public innovation process (centred on political manifestos and commitments) is by its nature centralised and episodic – a problem compounded by the structural limitations to innovation on the front line of service delivery.[2] One response to this has been to reduce the scope of the state, and parcel various activities and services out to contractors from the market and third sector – such as prisons, healthcare, adult education, and so on. But this trend has had its own problems.

If the state is to fully realise its potential as a critical force for the kind of social innovation required in the current period of transition, then there are profound structural issues that need to be addressed around how the state raises and allocates its funds, and how it is accountable for them. In this section we look at some of the devices that have been used to make public bureaucracies more creative and innovative. Some of the thinking here is set out in more detail in a series of publications on public innovation that have been published by the Young Foundation and NESTA.[3] We begin with some of the high level issues and then move onto more specific tools.

## Strategic issues

Innovation in the public sector always risks being a marginal add-on – small-scale in terms of funds, commitment of people and political capital. But serious innovation is closely tied into strategy. It is seen as a way to achieve outcomes more effectively, and to target issues that matter.

314) **Innovation linked into strategy.** Strategic considerations should drive a significant share of public innovation funding, specifically through: i) identifying priority issues, cost pressures, public concerns, and the fields where there are the biggest gaps between current performance and expectations; and ii) identifying in each field to what extent strategic goals can be met by adopting already proven innovations or developing new ones. For example, obesity is a major strategic challenge facing many governments, but there are very few proven models for reducing it. As a result there is little choice but to innovate.

315) **Visible leadership.** It matters greatly if leaders signal that innovation matters. President F.D. Roosevelt was an exemplar – saying publicly that he wanted to see experimentation, and sometimes failure, in order to solve public problems. Support from top officials is as important as from politicians. The UK government's top 200 civil servants spent their annual retreat in 2009 focused on innovation – a clear signal from their head that the agenda matters.

316) **Innovation needs to be supported by incentives,** or at least not blocked by disincentives. These will take different forms in different sectors. Systematic identification of key disincentives, and viability of alternatives, must be a priority for any public agency. Rewards can take the form of recognition, promotion or finance.

317) **Appropriate risk management.** Public agencies tend to be fearful of risk. The challenge is to manage risk, not eliminate it. Risk can be managed across a portfolio of projects that span the high return/high risk

end, as well as medium and low return agendas. A balanced view of risk is vital – some innovations spread too slowly but others spread too fast, without adequate evaluation and assessment, particularly when they win the backing of leaders. A commitment to evaluation and evidence, and staged development of new approaches, helps reduce risk.

318) **Formation and training** to integrate innovation into personal development, training, and culture. Some need to become specialists in spotting, developing and growing ideas. Others, particularly gatekeepers, need to know how to recognise the conditions for innovation. More generally, innovation, including a licence to take appropriate risks, should be part of personal development plans.

319) **Circuits of information** from users to front line staff and senior managers. The flow of information from the periphery to the centre is critical for learning, reviewing and improving. This can include online platforms to ensure rapid transmission of information. Examples include Patient Opinion and I Want Great Care – that hold service providers to account; or the Kafka Brigades in the Netherlands which research and solve problems in the public sector from the perspective of citizens and civil servants. Their objective is to cut bureaucratic red tape and help make Dutch society 'smarter' (see methods 17-21).

320) **User engagement** has been helped both by user groups themselves and by professional organisations providing methods for engaging citizens. Users play an important role in providing new insights into user needs, sometimes playing direct roles in redesigning services. Examples include expert patients, groups and mobilising ex-offenders in service design (see method 38).

321) **Learning cultures.** The biggest barrier to innovation is the lack of a culture of learning that rewards public agencies and public servants for learning from their own mistakes, learning from other sectors, and learning from other places. One feature of the most innovative public agencies is that they are comfortable adopting ideas from diverse and surprising sources.

322) **Safe spaces for innovation.** Examples include The 27e Region in France. There are 26 administrative regions in France. This virtual 27th 'region' is intended to provide the other regions with the space and opportunity to design and develop innovative approaches to policy. Its

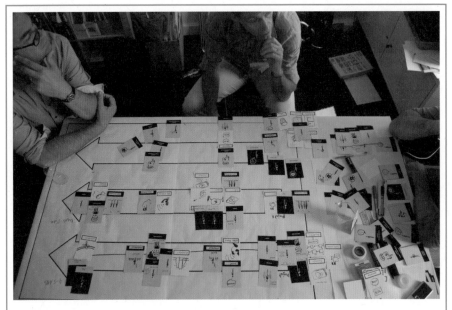

'Atelier 27' is a monthly workshop organised by The 27$^e$ Region with four to seven people, including civil servants from the Regions, politicians, experts, and citizens. Participants raise their own questions, and by the end of the day, are expected to produce visualized scenarios and proposals. Questions vary but have included: how can Regional decision making processes in the regeneration of old schools be improved? What would a city with 3,000 inhabitants look like in 2030? How would you go about introducing an environmentally-friendly tram (above)? More broadly, 'Atelier 27' aims to develop a culture of co-creation, creativity, design thinking and visualisation in public authorities. Image courtesy of The 27$^e$ Region.

goal is to foster creativity, social innovation and sustainability in public institutions, through community projects, prototyping, and design thinking.

## Public Finance: methods to generate internal innovation

The generation and adoption of innovation within the public sector depends on how money and accountability are organised – how public budgets are developed and agreed, and which structures of taxation and financial accountability promote rather than hinder innovation.

**Budgets to promote internal innovation**
The public sector has some well established tools for financing innovation beyond its borders, particularly through R&D funding for science and technology. But there are also many tools for encouraging staff to innovate, from managers to front line workers.

323) **'Top slicing'** departmental budgets for innovation, for example, 1 per cent of turnover as a rough benchmark (similar to the proportion of GDP now devoted to government support for technological and scientific research and development).

324) **Dedicated innovation funds** and internal public venture funds, such as the UK's 'Invest to Save' budget for cross-cutting innovations, The Enterprise Challenge in Singapore, and the $700 million US education innovation fund. In the UK, the NHS has established a £220 million innovation fund over five years to enable ideas to be developed and tested, with £20 million to be spent on a public competition for medical breakthroughs.

325) **Cross-cutting budgets** that support broad programmes which leave space for experiment and innovation, such as those for Sure Start.

326) **Outcome-based budgets** which can be used to promote innovation, giving greater freedom to providers to determine how they achieve outcomes, such as lower unemployment.

327) **Holistic local budgets** such as the New Deal for Communities, which gave local communities wide discretion on how to spend large sums of money (typically around £50 million over ten years), partly in order to accelerate innovation. One lesson from this experience was that setting budgets so high (partly to support big capital programmes) tended to bring with it a great deal of bureaucracy.

328) **Ring-fencing financial gains from innovation** for initiators and developers. Various devices have been developed to improve the incentives for innovation, particularly ones that deliver gains to other public agencies. These are easier to design for technologies than services, and bring all the problems associated with performance incentives, including deciding who in a team should benefit.

This playground at the Nunsmoor Centre in the West End of Newcastle is sure to be one the kids will love, because they designed it themselves. The costs were covered by Centre West with the support of Sure Start. Initially set up as part of the New Deal for Communities Scheme, Centre West continues to put the community in charge, ensuring the work continues even after government funding stops in 2010. Image courtesy of Andrew Hayward/Centre West.

329) **Online budget-setting tools.** An interesting example is the Australian website, Budget Allocator, which offers citizens the chance to shape municipal budgets.

330) **Sequencing in funding.** For example, starting with input targets (1 per cent of public service budgets to be committed to innovation), then progressing to outcome targets and more sophisticated ways of holding officials to account for both current performance and future performance (including innovation and adoption).

331) **Innovation-related pay** such as institutional, team and personal performance bonuses linked to innovation. These have been much discussed in many governments but have proven hard to operationalise, and like many bonus systems can lead to major problems of fairness (who was really responsible for the innovation?), and motivation. Japanese firms often have systems of collective bonuses for everyone, from the R&D team to secretaries and caretakers. They regard individual bonuses as divisive.

332) **Social clauses in public contracts,** for example, to promote innovative methods for employing unemployed people, those with disabilities or to reduce carbon footprints.

**Distributed accountability and democratic innovation**
Representative democracy took its current forms in the 19th century, with parliaments and assemblies, parties, regular elections, and in some countries manifestos and platforms. These models have become inadequate with the growing complexity of government – and representative democracy is increasingly being joined to participatory tools for engaging the public continuously in debate and decisions.

333) **Open forms of consultation and participation** such as the Peer-to-Patent Project in the US, which enables citizens to review and give advice on patent applications.[4] Other examples include deliberative polling techniques which solicit ideas and opinions from the public.

334) **Parliamentary structures to develop citizen ideas,** like Korea's Tribunus Plebis, a committee of senior legislators committed to putting citizen ideas into legislation.

335) **Open spaces to hold members of executive government to account.** President Obama's online 'town halls' let the public vote on which of the 106,000 questions submitted by the public he will respond to. Over the course of the first meeting, 1.7 million votes were counted.

336) **Participatory budgeting** enables citizens to define local priorities and allocate public money accordingly. Examples include the experiences of Ontario, Canada, Medellin, Colombia, Porto Alegre (Brazil) and several hundred others in Latin America and Europe. Through this style of budgeting, communities are actively engaged on policy issues, and governments and other organisations are allowed direct access to front line community needs.

The community decides. This is the Regional Participatory Budget Assembly in Partenon, Porto Alegre, Brazil. Local community members are voting on the priorities for 2010 and on the representatives for 2009-2010. Later, those representatives and the delegates vote on the budget during the meetings that take place after the end of the cycle of Assemblies, generally in September or October. Image courtesy of Ivo Gonçalves.

337) **Shadow budgeting processes** including budgets prepared by civil society. The Canadian Alternative Federal Budget (AFB) has been running since 1994 and is a joint initiative of the Canadian Centre for Policy Alternatives and CHO!CES.

338) **Grant allocation through public voting,** such as the ITV/Big Lottery Fund competition 'The People's 50 Million'. Another example is 'Help A London Park', an initiative launched by the Mayor of London to enable Londoners to decide which parks should receive funding for improvement.

339) **Opt-out rights for communities** to design and run their own services in place of existing state, regional, or national bureaucracies. These can be a powerful driver for innovation but also create issues of equity and efficiency (since they threaten economies of scale and scope). Some regeneration schemes (such as New Deal for Communities in the UK) have encouraged local communities to run their own housing maintenance and other services.

340) **Tracking public finances** may be aided by public balance sheet accounting and greater transparency of public finance (as happens in Estonia). Teams in several countries are working on ways to make public finance wholly transparent, with spending tagged to geographical areas, or groups. Total Place in the UK are piloting an atempt to map all spending in particular areas, in order to allow more creativity in thinking about how assets could be shared between agencies, or how actions by one agency could save money for another (for example, by providing more home-based care for older people to reduce pressures on hospitals). Another project, 'Where Does My Money Go?', set up by the Open Knowledge Foundation, is attempting to provide an interactive representation of UK public finance using maps, timelines, and other visualization techniques. New York's Open Book provides information on how New Yorkers' tax dollars are spent.

341) **Open-source auditing** as a mechanism for public accountability, using transparent access to public financial and other data.

342) **Audit and inspection regimes** which overtly assess and support innovation (the recent UK National Audit Office (NAO) report on innovation was a major step forward in rethinking audit as a support to innovation rather than a barrier to healthy risk-taking).

343) **Cross-government innovation metrics,** such as the Government Innovation Index developed by the Government of South Korea to measure current levels of innovation, and the results of new innovation.

**New forms of taxation and public revenue raising**
Taxation is often experienced as a forced levy in contrast to market exchange, but there has been a growth of experiments in the financing of collective goods, and the legitimation of tax, which encourage the kind of innovations that command public support. This is particularly the case in the environmental field, where charges on the basis of the 'polluter pays' encourage innovation in reducing pollution and materials (as with producer responsibility schemes), with a transfer of funds to those who have innovated (as in the UK's Landfill Allowance Trading Scheme).

344) **Hypothecated taxes** and obligations for households and corporations, such as the BBC licence fee, London Congestion Charge, Climate Change Levy, or Extended Producer Responsibility as in British Columbia.

345) **Tax variations** according to citizen involvement, for example giving tax reductions to households who participate in recycling programmes, and compensating for the loss of revenue by raising rates for non-participants. Tax rebates are increasingly used to promote public policies (such as Harlow's rate rebate for people insulating their homes).

346) **Voluntary taxes,** such as those introduced in Bogotá, Colombia, by the Mayor Antanas Mockus. Mockus asked citizens to pay an extra 10 per cent in voluntary taxes – 63,000 people did.

347) **One-off taxes** such as the Olympic levy on Londoners, or windfall taxes from utilities – for investment in emerging green technologies and other innovations.

348) **Community pledgebanks** are a development of the Pledgebank idea: citizens commit modest sums of money (e.g. $20) on the condition that a certain number of other citizens do so as well (e.g. 1000 people in a neighbourhood of 10,000). This creates a form of finance which sits halfway between taxation and charitable giving. Local government can also pledge to match such commitments.

349) **Transaction charges and payments,** including fees, variable charges, penalties, rewards, and hypothecated fees for services by the state.

350) **Public subscriptions, lotteries, and competitions** provide another source of funding for activities at one remove from the state. In some countries (e.g. New Zealand), lotteries provide a primary source of funding for community ventures.

351) **Socialising risk.** New forms of social insurance for long term care – for example, to create incentives for providers to develop innovative solutions which will reduce demand for services.

## Public mediums of exchange and means of payment

Most public finance is undertaken in national currencies. Public procurement and wages are paid in the relevant currency, and taxes are similarly raised in that form. But there have been a growing number of experiments with forms of payments which include tokens, or incentives in kind, or which consolidate citizens' public sector rights and obligations in personal public accounts, transferring public means of payment to them.

352) **Direct payments and personal service budgets,** such as the UK's direct payments scheme, and the extension of personal budgets to people with disabilities. Personal budgets are in use in US states such as Oregon and countries such as Sweden, and enable people to choose, arrange, and pay for their own care and services (see also method 183).

353) **Quasi-currencies** and environmental permits, such as Packaging Recovery Notes (PRNs) and emissions trading certificates, but also including targets, rewards, and penalties.

354) **Personal public accounts** for credits and debits such as the Danish NemKonto Easy Account. Here, Danish citizens and companies nominate one of their bank accounts as their NemKonto Account into which all payments to and from public institutions are directly transferred. Such accounts would enable the design of new public products, including loans and payments.

355) **Public smart cards** have been in use for over twenty years, and allow services to be reconfigured, often prompting innovative ways of thinking about services. Cards like the Hong Kong Octopus transit card or the London Oyster card have considerable potential for expansion.

356) **Loyalty and incentive schemes** can support and promote healthy and sustainable living. Examples include the joint Young Foundation/

Birmingham East and North Primary Care Trust (BEN PCT) 'Healthy Incentives' programme which provides points as rewards for healthy activities.

357) **Payment to citizens in the form of tokens,** such as the French ticket restaurants (a luncheon voucher scheme) in which the vouchers can now also be exchanged for fresh fruit and vegetables, or the recycling payments made in tokens in Curitiba, Brazil, that allow a certain number of free journeys on public transport and/or the purchase of food produced by local farmers.

358) **Local public currencies** such as the Wörgl in Austria during the 1930s, or more recently, the Patacón in Argentina. The key feature of these currencies is that the municipality or state not only pays labour through these notes, but accepts them for payment of taxes. In July 2009 the state of California, facing a severe budget deficit, agreed to accept IOUs issued to its creditors in payment of taxes, thereby creating the largest public secondary currency, of a kind previously vetoed by President Roosevelt in 1933.

**Public investment**

Financing public investment is complicated by the common difficulty in quantifying the effects of an investment, or capturing returns that are multi-dimensional and diffuse. This particularly applies to preventative investment. Private funding can be used where there are clear streams of revenue resulting from the investment, with the public funding element covering the wider social impact elements of an investment – and reducing risk.

359) **Local bonds,** including Tax Increment Financing (TIF) and Business Improvement Districts (BIDs). These create flows of resources at the local and very local levels, and can support new functions at arm's length from the local state.

360) **Generating revenue from public investment** on the US railroad model. Prior to investment, property rights are vested in a Community Land Trust (CLT) or public body which then benefits from the increased rental value of sites after the public investment has been undertaken. The Greater London Enterprise Board financed its operational expenditures for many years through the sale of industrial property it had bought during the recession of the early 1980s.

361) **Social investment funds,** such as the proposed Social Investment Bank to be funded from unclaimed bank accounts, which would act as a wholesaler for a range of financing needs (see method 475).

362) **Social enterprise investment funds,** such as the Social Enterprise Investment Fund launched by the UK's Department of Health with around £100 million, using a mix of loan and equity finance.

363) **Endowment finance** such as the National Endowment for Science, Technology and the Arts (NESTA) in the UK, or the various endowments established by the Canadian Government in the 2000s.

364) **Hybrid financing and joint ventures** such as the finance models used by Woking Borough Council and the London Climate Change Agency (LCCA) to develop sustainable energy programmes.

365) **Joint project financing** leveraging public money with voluntary contributions, sponsorship or community investment.

366) **Layered investments** combining tranches with different rates of risk/ return and different sources of capital (philanthropic, public, private) such as BlueOrchard (Switzerland) or Big Issue Invest in the UK:

367) **Scheduling returns** to ensure investors with the highest discount rates are given priority in the initial revenue flows from a project.

368) **Use of insurance** to quantify risk and reduce uncertainty for public bodies and investors. This is a particular issue with many environmental problems such as nuclear power or waste incineration. In some cases, insurance companies may even be urged to take responsibility, as with the Swiss Re insurance of pollution claims from landfill.

369) **Investment guarantees,** with any claim on the guarantee being paid out with a one year delay. This is to avoid the full value of the guarantee being counted in a public authority's current investment programme (Sheffield City Council pioneered this delayed payment method in the 1980s).

370) **Securitising future payment' streams to provide investment capital,** as with the Prime Carbon scheme in Australia which contracts sequestered carbon from microbial treatment of agricultural soils to large companies on a five year basis, allowing these payments to be

capitalised to fund farmers' investment. Similar measures could be used
to fund domestic or corporate energy efficiency measures.

371) **Financial instruments for preventative investment** including
the UK's 'Invest to Save' budget, the USA's Justice Reinvestment
programme, and contingent revenue bonds such as the proposed Social
Savings or Social Impact Bonds.

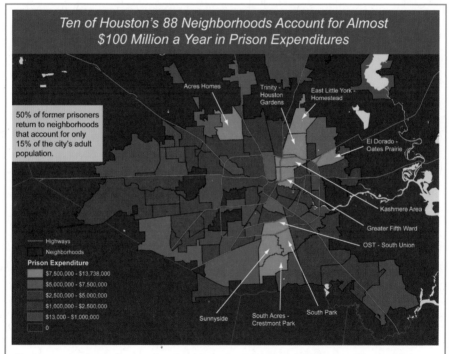

Justice reinvestment is a local approach to justice decision making which
seeks to reinvest some of the state funds spent on imprisonment into local
programmes that tackle the longer term causes of offending in specific
localities. It is based on geographic analyses of returning ex-offenders. The
analysis above, conducted by Eric Cadora at the Justice Mapping Center,
reveals that five counties accounted for more than half of the people
sentenced to prison at a cost to taxpayers of over half a billion dollars. Of
these localities, Harris County (Houston) received and contributed the most
prisoners, with ten of Houston's 88 neighbourhoods accounting for almost
$100 million a year in incarceration costs. This evidence is then used to target
preventative interventions more effectively. Image courtesy of Eric Cadora.

372) **Social Impact Bonds** are a financial tool being developed in the UK (by the Young Foundation) to provide a new way to invest money in social outcomes. They are part of a family of new financing devices aiming to capitalise social value, and provide better incentives for public agencies to make preventive investments. They were endorsed in a government white paper in December 2009.

373) **Health Impact Contracts** are a potential new financing device to connect the NHS in the UK with other agencies (primarily local government), with investments by local authorities (for example in home based care for the elderly) tied to future payments by the NHS – determined by whether the investment leads to lower pressure on hospitals and acute services.

374) **Bonus payments on spending** aligned to social outcomes such as the UK Government's Performance Reward Grant for local area partnerships.

375) **Public investment aimed at social innovation growth strategies** such as the proposed Social Investment Bank, the Toronto Atmospheric Fund, and Enterprise Boards.

376) **Public Finance Initiatives,** also referred to as 'public-private partnerships', have been mainly used to finance physical structures and infrastructures, from roads and school buildings to prisons. The initiatives were designed in part to bring in innovative models from the private sector.

**Fiscal moves to promote social innovation**
Favourable tax treatment is a means to incentivise innovation, not through the provision of investment funds but by lowering the cost of innovation, and improving prospective post-tax rates of return.

377) **Exemptions and assistance** such as tax relief along the lines of the Enterprise Investment Scheme (EIS) for social enterprises, or property tax holidays for early-stage social enterprise and charities.

378) **Experimental zones** are geographic areas which are used as a test bed for new ideas that can then be introduced nationwide. The main challenge with experimental zones is to balance experimentation and freedom with enough clarity about what is being experimented to ensure that the zones work well. Four experimental zones were set up in China

in the 1970s, to test out Deng Xiaoping's 'Open Door' policies. These zones provided a range of tax incentives to attract foreign investment and paved the way for the sweeping reforms and the unprecedented economic growth of the past three decades. More recently there have been experiments in health insurance in Chongqing, and democratic deliberative polling in the Wenling Municipality of Zhejiang Province. In the UK, experimental zones have been used with varying success. In the 1990s, Employment Zones allowed contractors to innovate new methods for getting unemployed people into work, with payment linked to outcomes rather than inputs and outputs.

379) **Differential tax, credits, allowances and estate duties for personal public investment,** such as those for higher education, elder care and environmental investment.

380) **Charitable status extended to allow tax allowances on investment funds,** as with charitable investment in Community Interest Companies, or the L3C model in the US which allows for programme-related investments from foundations.

381) **R&D tax credits** for the design and development of innovations. R&D tax credits have been extended to cover design, and although they are primarily designed for commercial companies, they could be adapted to fit the economics of social businesses.

## Legislation and regulation

Governments shape the conditions in which social entrepreneurs, businesses, non-profits, and others operate. In too many cases, good ideas clash with existing rules and regulations. However, new regulatory and legal frameworks (such as new standards, new legal forms and new planning requirements) can unleash creative forces and support social innovation.

382) **Policy instruments to re-make markets** to promote the social economy such as compulsory targets, including the employment of people with disabilities, regulations for renewable energy, fiscal measures, and planning conditions.

383) **Creation of new legal forms and requirements** such as Community Interest Companies (CICs) (see method 118) and the Charity Commission's public benefit test.

384) **Legal obligations** such as the NHS's 'Duty to Promote Innovation' placed on Strategic Health Authorities (SHAs).

385) **Planning and tax rules to promote creative economies** such as subsidised rent in art districts, including SoHo in New York and Hackney in London.

386) **Asset transfer programmes,** such as the UK Government's programme to pass buildings and other assets from government to community organisations.

## Raising incentives to innovate

Whether or not innovation becomes embedded within an organisation or department depends also on whether there is a culture which is supportive of new ideas. This requires clear signals from leadership that they want to see experimentation, backed up by incentives and structures of support that enable this to take place, as well as organisational cultures that support interaction across organisational boundaries (and time for engagement and cross-pollination), and protected time for reflection.

387) **Integrating innovation into personal appraisal** for civil servants, including 360 degree innovation appraisals.

388) **Innovation capability assessment,** such as the 'capability reviews' which judge all national departments in the UK and compare their performance publicly.

389) **Innovation reports** provide regular assessments of how well public agencies are supporting innovation and adopting innovations from elsewhere. The UK's Strategic Health Authorities will report annually from 2010 onwards.

390) **Innovation awards** play a critical role in highlighting innovative programmes and projects within government. One prominent example is the Innovations in American Government Awards programme, organised by the Ash Institute for Democratic Governance and Innovation at Harvard University's John F. Kennedy School of Government. Through its prestigious annual awards competition, the programme has served to highlight innovative projects within fields as diverse as youth justice, environmental management, education, public health and e-governance,

and acted as a catalyst for continued innovation in dealing with some of society's most pressing public concerns.

"Many past winners of The Innovations in American Government Awards have influenced reform and serve as harbingers for today's national legislation," said Stephen Goldsmith, Director of the Innovations in American Government Program. "Notable past winners include CompStat, New York City's crime reduction tool, and One Church One Child, Illinois's minority church and adoption agency collaboration." Since 1986, the Innovations in American Government Awards have recognised over 400 public sector initiatives that have led to innovative practices that benefit citizens. Throughout its history, the programme has generated a wealth of research based on award-winning government

Ash Center Director, Anthony Saich; Secretary of Housing and Urban Development, Shaun Donovan; Innovations in Government Director Stephen Goldsmith; and New York City Acquisition Fund Team at 2008 Innovations in American Government Awards ceremony in Washington, D.C.

New York City's Acquisition Fund is a $230 million partnership that finances the purchase of land and buildings for affordable housing. It was one of the winners of the 2008 Innovations in American Government Awards. Image courtesy of Sam Kittner.

innovations and the study of how innovation occurs. More than 450 Harvard courses and over 2,250 courses worldwide have incorporated Innovations in American Government case studies, including Milano Graduate School, University of West Indies, and the Hong Kong Polytechnic University. The Ford Foundation is a founding donor of the Innovations in American Government Awards.

South Africa set up the Centre for Public Service Innovation (CPSI) in 2002 and now runs regular awards. There are similar awards in various countries including Brazil and Denmark.

## Innovation from the workforce

The close involvement of the workforce in innovation has been a feature of Toyota's methods of work organisation that has spread to manufacturing and service industries over the past 25 years. Similar practices are now being introduced into some spheres of public service (notably in healthcare) as well as closer engagement with trade unions in the improvement of service quality.

391) **Public sector unions,** as sources of innovation and promoters of faster adoption. In some fields, unions representing professionals and manual workers have resisted innovations (particularly ones involving changes to demarcations). However, in other cases, unions have helped drive innovation, such as the Fire Brigades Union in the UK which helps firemen find part-time employment as benefits advisors alongside their roles as firemen, or the local branch of Unison in Newcastle upon Tyne that played a central role in the introduction of a new IT system for the Council. In Norway, the model municipalities initiative involves politicians, management and trade unions in a quality programme for upgrading public services.

392) **Supporting front line workers as innovators** such as the joint IDEO/ Kaiser Permanente (KP) project in the US. Shift changes were identified as one of the biggest challenges to continuity of patient care. When nurses go on or off shift they need to exchange information to ensure patient safety and quality of care. But it is easy for information to be lost or inaccurately transferred. So, IDEO convened a series of brainstorm sessions with nurses, doctors and other health professionals, after a couple of weeks of intense observation in one of Kaiser Permanente's hospital wards. The nurses were then involved in designing and testing a series of prototypes to try out alternative methods of exchanging

information. These prototypes were refined and adapted as a result of feedback from the nurses. The new system proved very successful and has now been implemented in every ward in 35 KP hospitals.

393) **Tithes of working time** to generate collaborative public innovation – an extension of the Google model where engineers are encouraged to spend 20 per cent of their time developing their own projects. The parallels in the public sector include initiatives making it easier for teachers or lecturers to take sabbaticals (as in Canada), or freeing up time for public sector workers to volunteer for socially innovative projects.

394) **Secondments** of public sector employees into 'skunk works', innovation teams, and projects to develop service innovation.

395) **Greater freedoms in designated or priority areas** as a spur for innovation. Examples include the 'Power to Innovate', introduced in 2003 in the UK to allow schools, colleges, local authorities and trusts to ask the Minister to suspend or modify educational legislation that was holding back innovative approaches to raising standards. In this case, the impact was relatively modest – in the first five years of the programme, 24 orders were made affecting 199 schools. They were limited to issues such as the timing of school sessions (half of them), changes in school governance – such as the size of the governing body or pupil representation (one third), and the provision of free school meals. However, the model could be applied in other contexts.

396) **Innovation animators.** As part of the model municipalities initiative (see above), Trondheim municipality in Norway has created a team of 30 part time innovation animators, who work for a day a week with the public workforce to develop innovative service ideas.

397) **Secure employment innovation models** which separate project failure from redundancy. Examples include funding a range of parallel projects to test out innovations with job security, so that individuals can be transferred from failures to successes.

398) **Accreditation, search and recruitment of public innovators** by commercial headhunters or government agencies. For example, with accredited lists of individuals with proven track records who can be quickly employed onto projects. The Neighbourhood Renewal advisers in the UK are one example.

## Inside-outside collaboration

An important area of public sector innovation has been to encourage collaboration between public service workers and civil society, and make the boundaries between them more fluid.

399) **Inside-outside teams** linking civil servants with social entrepreneurs and those working with communities, as in Ontario's Community Economic Development programme in the 1990s. Such teams can also be formed to advance particular innovation projects, with their own funding, as a form of public venturing.

400) **Volunteering in the public sector.** Encouraging volunteering within the public sector (for example in health, education and care), to bring in new perspectives as well as energies. Parents volunteering in schools are a common example. Around 500,000 volunteers contribute to the UK NHS.

401) **Secondments** of public sector employees to community organisations and private enterprises, and vice versa.

402) **Collaborative structures for more innovative service design and delivery** – such as Denmark's School, Social Services and Policy Cooperation Scheme (SSP) for preventing juvenile crime, which has contributed to one of the world's most successful systems for reducing and preventing crime, along with low prison rates.

**End notes**

1. See Moore, M.H. (1995) 'Creating Public Value: Strategic Management in Government.' Cambridge, MA: Harvard University Press; Wainwright, H. (2009) 'Public Service Reform But Not As We Know It.' Hove: Picnic; IDeA (2005) 'Innovation in public services: literature review.' London: IDeA; Mulgan, G. and Albury, D. (2003) 'Innovation in the public sector.' London: Cabinet Office. The former provides the following typology of public sector innovation: (i) policy innovations (new missions, objectives, strategies); (ii) service or product innovations (new features and design of services); (iii) delivery innovations (new ways of delivering services and interacting with service users); (iv) process innovations (new internal procedures and organisational forms); and (v) system innovations (including governance structures).
2. Murray, R. (2009) 'Danger and Opportunity: Crisis and the new Social Economy.' Provocation. London: NESTA.
3. See for example, Murray, R. op.cit.; Mulgan, G. (2007) 'Ready or Not? Taking Innovation in the Public Sector Seriously.' London: NESTA; Bacon, N. *et al.* (2008) 'Transformers: How local areas innovate to address changing social needs.' London: NESTA.
4. Noveck, B.S. (2008) Wiki Government: how open-source democracy can make government decision-making more expert and more democratic. 'Democracy Journal.' No. 7, Winter 2008.

# 2 SUPPORT IN THE GRANT ECONOMY

Civil society and the grant economy are the most common sites of social innovation – in campaigns, social movements, non-governmental organisations and associations. By its nature this sector tends to be fragmented and small in scale. But its sense of mission often means that it is better than other sectors in acting holistically, and better at linking action to advocacy.[1]

Many new methods and tools have been developed to support and grow promising ideas. However, this sector is generally better at creating ideas than changing whole systems. The more recent waves of interest in social entrepreneurship and venture philanthropy have also been better at supporting individual projects than making them more than the sum of their parts, which usually involves collaboration across sectoral boundaries.

We describe this sector as the grant economy because grants play an important part, even though much of the income received within this sector comes from other sources, such as contracts with governments and other kinds of trading income.

Despite this breadth of sources the main challenges for the sector are growth, and the reliability of funding sources. Individual donors can be unpredictable. Institutional donors tend to avoid long term commitments, and prefer funding start-ups. Grants are cost based, and do not allow for the generation of internal surpluses that can finance growth. Many grant givers have a preference for projects and programmes, and are reluctant to provide core funding. Grant-aided organisations are often the first to suffer in state budget cuts and economic recessions. Grant programmes throughout the developed world complain of a lack of sustainable grant funding.[2]

Commissions and contracts have tended to grow as a source of income (and account for 30-40 per cent of income in most developed countries). A much smaller, but visible, trend has been the growth in venture philanthropy, with much greater involvement of donors in projects and organisations. Another has been the spread of online platforms which enable individuals to support particular projects.

These developments are transforming the sector. To quicken the pace of change and encourage the generation and adoption of innovation within the grant economy, there need to be new kinds of finance, platforms, packages of support, and regulatory, governance and accountability frameworks. There is a key role to be played by government and charitable foundations in re-shaping these structures.[3]

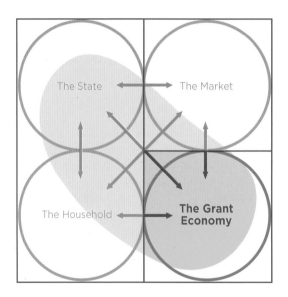

## Finance

Philanthropic grants should be the ideal funding for social innovation. Donors can handle high levels of risk, and do not need the certainty of returns of the private sector. Yet there has been surprisingly little attention to how finance could best support innovation, and what mix of funding for individuals, teams and enterprises works best, or how to stage funding to maximum effect. We anticipate rapid evolution in this space as philanthropists develop more sophisticated hybrid tools that can combine grants, loans, and equity.

Here, we focus on grants and the relationship between donors and recipients. For more methods see 'commissioning and procurement' (see methods 170-183) for ways in which the public sector can support innovation within the grant economy.

### Grant giving

Increasingly, donors are trying to avoid some of the limitations of traditional grant funding. Some are using prize funds to catalyse innovations and others are treating grants more like investments – alongside project involvement, technical support, continuous funding, and the coverage of core costs.[4]

403) **Direct funding for individuals,** including the grants given by UnLtd, The Skoll Foundation, and Ashoka.

404) **Award and recognition prizes** are intended to celebrate or mark a person or organisation's achievement. These tend to be awarded after the fact, such as the Nobel Prizes. These prizes have become increasingly popular over the last decade for rewarding social entrepreneurs, non-profit organisations, and others working in the field of philanthropy. There are now some 25 philanthropic organisations offering awards worldwide, such as the Skoll Awards for Social Entrepreneurship, the Social Entrepreneur of the Year Award (organised by the Schwab Foundation for Social Entrepreneurship), and the MacArthur Fellows Program which grants $500,000 to recipients over five years. Such awards can be an effective means of distributing funds to already established social entrepreneurs.[5] A criticism sometimes made of these methods is that they tend to favour internationally networked individuals rather than grass roots innovators.

405) **Fast grants** such as those distributed by the Sobrato Family Foundation which has reduced bureaucracy to ensure that grantees receive funds quickly.

406) **Term-limited charities** are required to spend down assets within a particular timeframe. One example is the John M. Olin Foundation, another is Atlantic Philanthropies.

407) **Competitions and challenge funds** can be an effective means of spurring social innovation. The X Prize Foundation, for example, have offered $10 million to the first team to produce a device capable of accurately sequencing 100 human genomes within ten days – at a cost of no more than $10,000 per genome. If successful, this technology would mark nothing less than a revolution by truly personalising medical care. A similar revolution in the car industry is the hope for the Progressive Automotive X Prize. Below is one of the registered entries.

Recently, the X Prize Foundation have partnered with the Bill and Melinda Gates Foundation to tackle difficulties in treating tuberculosis and a new two stage Village Utility X Prize aims to bring drinking water, renewable energy, and connectivity to villages in the developing world.

The Progressive Automotive X Prize: teams must produce a low-carbon, low-polluting car which drives at least 100 miles per gallon. Upstream pollutants are taken into account and the car cannot generate more than 200 grams of $CO_2$ per mile. In addition, the teams have to prepare business plans which demonstrate how the car can be taken to market immediately. This is the West Philly Hybrid X Team, a group of students from West Philadelphia High School's Academy of Automotive and Mechanical Engineering with their entry, the EVX. Image courtesy of the West Philly Hybrid X Team.

408) **Intermediaries** who allocate grants for specific projects on behalf of the donor, for example in the cultural sector.

409) **Micro R&D grants** for concept development and prototyping.

410) **Initial Public Offerings (IPOs)** originally used by companies to sell shares to the public, are now used by non-profit organisations to secure longer-term funding with a detailed pledge to provide a social return on the 'investment'. This technique is employed by Do Something, College Summit, and Teach for America.

411) **Grants as investment** including tapered grant funding, public equity, and preference shares.

412) **Grants as complements** to innovation investment packages. Grant funding for off-balance sheet expenditure, for example Cordaid's investment and development packages for commodity development projects, or the UK's Department for International Development (DFID) Frich grant programme for UK market development for African supply chains.

413) **Inverse tapering: grant growth based on performance.** Organisations that advise donors and funders how to give more effectively and closely monitor the performance of the charities with which they are engaged. New Philanthropy Capital in the UK and Geneva Global in the US perform this role.

414) **Giving and social investment** circles such as the Funding Network, United Way, Social Venture Network, or the North Virginian Giving Circle of HOPE (Helping Other People Everydy). The last of these has over 100 members, who in four years have awarded over $200,000, and contributed 3,500 hours of voluntary time to community projects.

415) **Social innovation partnerships:** tax holidays and contributions in kind.

**Improving the grant relationship**
There are a range of intermediaries and online platforms which are attempting to improve the relationship between those giving and those receiving grants, often by linking the two together in more efficient and effective ways. In this field, the web offers new ways to cut costs and widen connections. Websites like Kiva, which connect donors with social entrepreneurs, have already been

making these links. Experiments in 'crowdfunding' potentially enrich the gift relationship, and democratise the sector's source of finance.

416) **Intermediaries for contributions in kind** provide labour and skills matching for volunteering, such as the Taproot Foundation's Service Grant programme which provides not-for-profit organisations with pro bono marketing, human resources and IT consulting services.

417) **Philanthropic 'eBays'.** Philanthropic platforms such as VolunteerMatch which help people find volunteering opportunities in their local area.

418) **Donor platforms,** such as GlobalGiving, Altruistiq Exchange, Network for Good, Firstgiving and Guidestar. Internet donor sites dramatically reduce the cost of fundraising (estimated at between 15 per cent and 33 per cent of funds raised in the US). We can expect similar websites to develop features like donor forums, star ratings, Good Giving Guides and Amazon type links (those who have given to x have also given to y and z).

## Mission-related investment

Philanthropy has increasingly moved to softening the distinction between grant and investment – viewing funds as supporting projects that contribute to a specific mission, including transformations of whole sectors for social ends.

419) **Strategic investments to transform sectoral provision,** for example, the Bill and Melinda Gates Foundation's investment in small high schools across America; and the Prosperity Initiative; which creates sectoral partnerships to stimulate industries that create income and employment for the rural poor.

420) **Venture philanthropy** focused on innovation in particular sectors, such as the Robert Wood Johnson Foundation's (RWJF's) Pioneer Portfolio which specialises in health and IT.

421) **Philanthropic mutual funds** such as the Acumen Fund and the Global Fund for Women.

Processing bamboo as part of Prosperity Initiative's plan to transform the bamboo sector in North-West Vietnam. In two years the project has enabled 22,000 people to move out of poverty. The project's goal is to move 750,000 people out of income poverty across Vietnam, Lao PDR and Cambodia by 2020. Image courtesy of the Prosperity Initiative.

## Governance and accountability

Too often within the grant economy, governance and accountability structures do not resonate with the organisation's social mission. And, in the UK at least, there are often questions about who a charitable or non-profit organisation is accountable to. Some organisations circumvent these questions by actively engaging beneficiaries and users in decision making processes. Here are a few ways how.

422) **User and beneficiary representation on management boards.**
One example is Room 13, which started in Scotland in 1994 when a group of students set up their own visual arts studio. The students work

A management committee meeting at Room 13 in Old Ford School, Tower Hamlets. The board is made up of children who are responsible for running the art studio and raising funds. Image courtesy of Old Ford School Room 13.

with an artist in residence, learning and experimenting with new ideas and approaches. The students are responsible for running the studio and raising funds. In this way, it combines creative freedom, business practice, and collaborative learning. The idea has spread and there are now Room 13 studios in Mexico, Nepal, Austria, South Africa, USA, Turkey, Holland, China, and Canada. Room 13 artists have exhibited at the Tate Modern in London, at the National Gallery in Edinburgh, organised trips to India and Everest Base Camp. There is an annual International Summer School.

423) **Innovation assessments** commissioned to assess the views of users and beneficiaries, and whether the innovation itself and the process surrounding it meet their needs.

424) **Members and associates** as sources of innovation and review, providing independent perspectives.

425) **Metrics for venture philanthropy** such as those developed by Homeward Bound, a project to end homelessness in the US, or 'blended value' measures and 'social return on investment' measures used for stakeholder communications (for more information on metrics see methods 208-229).

426) **Effective philanthropy methods,** encompass many tools for feedback and assessment including those developed by the Center for Effective Philanthropy which allow recipients to rate philanthropic foundations.

427) **Providing extensive information on NGO performance,** such as Guidestar's services and databases in many countries worldwide, and New Philanthropy Capital in the UK.

## Packages of support

A network of support services for grant-based organisations has developed, some are specialist private firms, some are social enterprises, and some are charities themselves. They provide legal and business advice, offer free mentoring services, and help to raise funds.

428) **Support services for innovators** including mentoring, information and advice, connections and networks, and public visibility, such as Cleveland's Civic Innovation Lab in Michigan and the Social Innovation Generator in Toronto, Canada. ·

429) **Capacity-building support.** Venture philanthropists, including Private Equity Foundation and Impetus Trust, are now using the skills of the private equity industry to help 'turn around' charities and build their internal capacities. The Private Equity Foundation has already worked with more than 30 charities in the UK.

## Training and formation

Some studies have highlighted the need for skills and formation within the grant economy and identified a lack of training and experience as one of the main barriers to the sector's success. Leaders of non-profit organisations, charities, associations and foundations have to contend with the challenges

Teaching an UpRising. UpRising is a youth leadership programme based in London, created by the Young Foundation. Here, UpRisers are taking part in a learning session at the Roffey Park Leadership Retreat. Each UpRiser presents on an issue affecting their local community and receives feedback from other UpRisers. These sessions are intended to spark ideas about the community campaigns UpRisers carry out as part of the course. Image courtesy of the Young Foundation.

of financial sustainability and stakeholder management while keeping the organisation aligned to its mission and values.

430) **Developing skills within the grant economy.** In the UK, ACEVO and the NCVO provide a range of training programmes for non-profit organisation managers in order to develop capacity within the sector. There are also small-scale training providers such as Islington and Camden Training Network – which provide tailored, hands on support to voluntary and community groups in their local areas.

431) **Personal assessment tools** to understand capacities for leadership and entrepreneurship, such as Echoing Green's SEQ – social emotional

intelligence – model. Many programmes now include a strong emphasis on self-knowledge and development.

432) **Training for social entrepreneurs,** such as Echoing Green in the US, the School for Social Entrepreneurs in the UK, and Fuping in China (see also 'training and formation' in the market economy, methods 483-487). Many MBAs now offer modules on social entrepreneurship, and there is a thriving market in specialist courses.

433) **Training for future leaders.** One example is the Clore Social Leadership Programme which helps to develop future third sector leaders in the UK. Another example in the UK is UpRising, a new leadership programme being developed by the Young Foundation to support and train a new generation of civic innovators and community organisers. During the year long course, each participant designs and undertakes a community campaign of their choice.

434) **Secondments.** One new example is the 'exchange programme' being set up by the Social Innovation Exchange (SIX). Two people from two different organisations would swap roles for between three and six months. It is a way of tapping into an organisation's knowledge and networks, while exposing members of staff to new working cultures and experiences.

## Legislation and Regulation

Grant-based organisations operate within a set of laws and regulations which affect their capacity to grow and be financially resilient. They may be given exemptions from some types of tax, for example, but only recently have there been moves to develop new types of company structure, and wider scope for charity operations.

435) **Planning and tax rules to promote creative economies** such as subsidised rent in arts districts, including SoHo in New York and Hackney in London, or the waiving of tax on businesses setting up in the favelas of Curitiba in Brazil (see method 385).

436) **Legal forms and requirements** such as Community Interest Companies, or the Charity Commission's public benefit test which gives social purpose organisations various tax exemptions, and require

existing charities to demonstrate their public value.

437) **Propertising commons** and distributing the rents for social purposes. Giving assets to a community land trust, or vesting new knowledge in a foundation, are examples.

## Networks

Civil society has become increasingly effective in creating its own networks to share ideas and support innovation.

438) **Global networks** such as Civicus, an international alliance dedicated to strengthening citizen action and civil society throughout the world. It works at the local, national and regional level, with organisations including non-governmental organisations, trade unions, faith-based networks, professional associations, non-profit capacity development organisations, philanthropic foundations and other funding bodies, businesses, and social responsibility programmes.

439) **National networks** such as NCVO or SCVO in the UK, many of which run programmes to encourage their members to innovate.

440) **Networks of recipients** such as those promoted by the EU EQUAL programme, which brought together grant recipients to share experiences and best practice, and disseminate information about their projects.

441) **Networks providing inspirations and links** such as WiserEarth which includes an online directory of non-governmental and socially responsible organisations. It now includes over 110,000 entries from 243 countries, territories, and sovereign islands. Another example is Worldchanging, a series of books and a website which includes tens of thousands of stories about new tools, models and ideas for building a 'bright green' future.

### End notes

1. Blackmore, A. (2006) 'How voluntary and community organisations can help transform public services.' London: NCVO.
2. Thomson, L. and Caulier-Grice, J. (2007) 'Improving Small Scale Grant Funding for Local, Voluntary and Community Organisations.' London: Young Foundation.
3. There is a huge literature, mostly from the USA about managing non-profits. See, for example, Drucker, P. (1990) 'Managing the Non-profit Organisation.' New York: HarperCollins.
4. John, R. (2006) Venture Philanthropy: the evolution of high engagement philanthropy in Europe. 'Skoll Centre for Social Entrepreneurship Working Paper.' Oxford: Saïd Business School, University of Oxford. Available at: http://www.sbs.ox.ac.uk/centres/skoll/research/Documents/Venture%20Philanthropy%20in%20Europe.pdf. For large scale developments in this field, see: Bishop, M. and Green, M. (2008) 'Philanthrocapitalism.' London: A&C Black.
5. Kasper, G. and Clohesy, S. (2008) 'Intentional Innovation: how getting more systematic about innovation could improve philanthropy and increase social impact.' A paper for the W.K. Kellogg Foundation.

# 3 SUPPORT IN THE MARKET ECONOMY

The boundaries between the private sector and the social sector are breaking down for many reasons. They include the continued growth of social industries – such as health, education and care. Social provision has also been opened up to business in many countries. And business has increasingly seen engagement in social issues as a source of new ideas, reputation, and recruitment. Many businesses now see social innovation as a field for creating new business opportunities: for growing brand equity (through association with well known charities or social enterprises); attracting talent (particularly younger people who want to believe that their employer has a social conscience); and to stimulate cultures of innovation in the mainstream business through engagement with different types of organisation.

The most significant development has been in the growth of social enterprises. These are businesses which earn a profit but are focussed on their social goals.[1] The main challenge for social enterprises is to maintain their commercial position in the market whilst staying true to their social goals. Many, being small, lack economies of scale and scope. Where their innovations are successful, larger commercial organisations will tend to enter their markets and swamp them (as has been the case with organic food, fair trade and recycling). In some cases, clusters of social enterprises have developed a network for collaboration and joint services which has enabled them to access services – normally available only to large firms – while remaining small themselves. Increasingly though, there are examples of social enterprises establishing themselves in the mainstream.

Inspirational examples and more information on successful business models

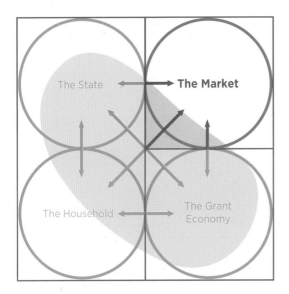

are critical for the growth and sustainability of the social enterprise sector. There need to be more diversified capital markets, packages of support for social entrepreneurs, and more supportive regulatory and legislative frameworks. More broadly, business leaders also need to become aware of the growing importance of values to their business.

## Social business models

Social business models are enabling organisations to tap into new sources of funding, and organise governance and accountability structures in a way that resonates with the mission of the organisation (see also methods on ownership and organisational form in the Sustaining section in Part 1).

442) **Social enterprises** operate in the market to achieve social goals. There is currently no universally accepted definition of social enterprise. This is because social enterprises can take numerous forms, are engaged in multiple spheres of activity, and because legal structures vary from country to country. For example, in Italy, social enterprises are constrained by a non-distribution clause – that is, all income has to be reinvested in the enterprise. In the UK, the Community Interest Company (CIC) was created as a new legal form in 2004 to reduce the tensions between finance and mission. CIC status makes the social mission dominant, and limits the returns on capital. There is an asset

lock, which means that any asset sale must be at market value, or transferred to another CIC or charity, so that any increase in value is retained for the benefit of 'the community of interest'. There is also a limit on dividends of 35 per cent of profits. The term also covers a wide range of organisations from co-operatives to public service providers, and from community/voluntary associations to 'work insertion' organisations, and companies limited by guarantee.

Social enterprises can generate income in a myriad ways. Some may generate their income through direct provision of a service which helps meet their social or environmental objectives. For example, Turning Point in the UK provides – among other things – rehabilitation services for those affected by drugs or alcohol. Others sell goods and services to customers while working towards their objectives behind the scenes, such as the Archipelago Cooperative which came out of the San Patrignano rehabilitation community in Rimini, Italy, or the Big Issue,

This is a Big Issue salesman in Bendigo, Australia. The Big Issue is a street magazine sold by homeless people. The magazine is now sold in the UK, Australia, Japan, South Africa, Kenya, Ethiopia, Malawi, and Namibia. Image courtesy of Michael Valli.

which is a magazine sold by homeless people.

443) **Social enterprise mutuals** as providers of joint services for their members, such as the service consortia in the, Third Italy, or Work Ventures in Australia.

444) **Consumer co-ops** such as the Japanese food co-ops which have 13 million members. They are organised around box distribution schemes, which have enabled them in some cases to outcompete local supermarkets and force their closure.

445) **Hybrid businesses with social missions built into governance,** such as Banca Intesa, the Co-operative Bank and Welsh Water.

446) **For-profit development of new social models,** for example welfare-to-work services, prisoner rehabilitation or disability services.

447) **Extending the co-operative economy in production,** including MONDRAGON and Peruvian coffee co-ops.

448) **Foundations as owners of corporations,** such as the Bertelsmann Foundation and the Robert Bosch Foundation. This model – primarily found in Germany – creates a different dynamic from those which give part of a company's profits to a separate foundation, or the US model where an entrepreneur becomes rich through one business and then puts a proportion of their personal wealth into a separate foundation.

## Social business partnerships

There are also a variety of ways in which businesses can engage with social innovation. Some are more 'hands on' – such as the provision of services for social good – and others are more 'hands off' – such as providing resources such as proprietary technology.

449) **Corporate social responsibility (CSR)** that involves a mix of grant giving, volunteering and, in some cases, social uses of marginal business assets, such as Salesforce's provision of software to non-profit organisations, or TNT's distribution of food to disaster areas.

450) **Hybrid business models that combine business capacities with**

M-PESA allows people to transfer money using a mobile phone. The term M-PESA comes from a combination of 'M' for mobile and 'Pesa' meaning money in Swahili. It is a joint partnership between Safaricom and Vodafone. Kenya was the first country in the world to use this service. Image courtesy of Vodafone.

**social goals** such as Vodafone's M-PESA mobile banking service in Kenya, using capacity on mobile phones to provide cheap and safe transactions for the unbanked. M-PESA now has half a million users in London in addition to its users in east Africa.

451) **Corporate not-for-profit management of social provision** such as Academy Schools in the UK and Charter Schools in the US.

452) **Partnerships between social enterprises and corporations** with not-for-distributed profits such as BASF-GAIN initiative for vitamin A in Africa, the Danone-Grameen yoghurt enterprise in Bangladesh and the BASF – Grameen venture, also in Bangladesh, which hopes to improve health and business opportunities for those on low income in the country.

453) **Market commitments** such as Cadbury's commitment to buy only fairtrade cocoa for one of its products.

454) **Business engagement in service evaluation,** for example the Azim Premji Foundation (and offshoot of WIPRO) financing large-scale trials of alternative models for running schools in India.

455) **Social uses of commercial technology** – such as IBM's use of translation software on its Meedan website of Arabic blogs, or Dialogue Café and the Social Innovation Exchange (SIX) using TelePresence technology developed by Cisco.

# Finance

One of the big challenges for social enterprise is growth. Partly, this is because they face limited access to risk and growth capital, and to highly specialist technical knowledge, but it is also a reflection of the fact that as social enterprises grow, they often face difficulties in balancing conflicting pressures. Much has been written about social returns on investment, triple bottom lines and 'blended value'[2] but how to ensure that the interests of investors remains subordinate to the social mission remains a critical question for social enterprise.

## Social finance

Increasingly, there are a range of financial instruments and packages which take into account the particular needs of social enterprises and businesses with social goals. A number of these, like public share issues, funding through co-operative subscription and crowdfunding are discussed in section 4 on Sustaining. Here we look at other emerging channels of social finance.

456) **Ethical investing,** also known as 'socially responsible investing', covers a broad range of financing strategies which seek to maximise both social and financial returns on investment – or at least, reduce the negative impacts of investments. Investments can be screened negatively – to exclude, for example, companies and organisations which are responsible for exploitative labour practices, cause harm to people and planet or are at odds with the values and mission of the investing organisation. So, for example, companies which pollute, or sell and manufacture weapons, alcohol and tobacco are avoided. Investments can also be screened positively to include companies which further social and environmental goals. For example, the Norwegian Government Pension Fund follows a series of ethical guidelines issued by the Ministry of Finance – these include the stipulation that the fund cannot make investments which 'may contribute to unethical acts of omissions, such

as violations of fundamental humanitarian principles, serious violations of human rights, gross corruption or severe environmental damages'. The website Your Ethical Money provides advice on how to direct personal investment into green, sustainable and ethical products.

457) **Mission-connected investment** is a form of ethical investing – it allows organisations to tie their investments closely to their missions in order to achieve their charitable goals. So, for example, an environmental foundation might choose to invest in recycling and renewable energy companies, while foundations dedicated to alleviating poverty might choose to invest in microfinance and fair trade.

458) **Social enterprise funds** including the new venture capital fund, set up by Triodos Bank, which invests in high impact and commercially sustainable social enterprises. Their aim is to help grow a dozen or so social enterprises in the UK.

459) **Social venture funds** that use equity-like investments for start-up and early-stage social ventures where loan financing is unsuitable. Examples include Bridges Community Ventures in the UK, which invests in businesses based in regeneration areas and in sustainable business sectors, including the environment, education, and healthcare.

460) **Microcredit for microproduction.** Grameen, BRAC and ASA in Bangladesh, and the multiple versions of microcredit inspired by them, as well as much older traditions of microcredit in Europe. Triodos Bank, in the UK, has invested in the microfinance sector since 1994. The Bank now has a total of €140 million lent and invested in 80 Microfinance Institutions in 35 countries, across Africa, Latin America, Asia, and Eastern Europe.

461) **Peer-to-peer lending.** One example is Kiva, the world's first micro-lending website which enables individuals to lend small sums of money to entrepreneurs on low incomes.

462) **Charitable loans** such as those provided by Charity Bank, the only bank in the UK which is a registered charity. They lend well below the market rate to charities and other social purpose organisations.

463) **Charitable Bonds** such as those developed in the UK by Citylife. These bonds enable investors to release 20 per cent of the value of their

investment for charity, and for those paying off loans – all the interest goes to charity as well. Another variant enables housing associations to get loans from a community and pay it back over five years at 20 per cent interest with all the interest going to mission-aligned charities as a donation.

464) **Charitable equity.** In the UK it has recently been agreed that charities can invest in the start-up equity of social ventures, as with the Mustard Seed charity's investment in the fair trade Community Interest Company, Liberation Foods.

465) **Investment-readiness support** aims to get projects or promising enterprises to a stage where traditional investors can make investments. This can include, for example, providing interim finance directors or accelerating product or service testing, in order to allow loan and equity providers to come in. Other useful elements include standardised due diligence packs (business plan, accounts, legal information, etc) to enable approaches to any funder.

466) **Philanthropic investment for growth** such as the CAN Breakthrough Social Investment Fund which provides strategic support and growth capital to established social enterprises with the ambition and potential, both to scale up their businesses and maximise their social impact. Breakthrough was founded by CAN (formally known as Community Action Network) and the private equity firm Permira in 2005. CAN, founded in 1998, runs CAN Social Investment, leveraging business support from leading private sector companies, as well as CAN Mezzanine, which provides shared office space for more than 115 charities and social enterprises in sites in central London (see also method 487).

467) **R&D mentored funding prior to start-up lending,** such as MONDRAGON's Caja Laboral. The MONDRAGON group is now the third largest industrial group in Spain – it has built up a network of 140 worker co-operatives and employs over 100,000 people. The network's bank, the Caja Laboral, provides credit to the co-ops that it helps to set up, but it also provides extensive forms of technical support while the co-ops are developing.

**Social finance institutions**

There are also a range of organisations and institutions which are now catering to the specific needs of social enterprises and businesses with social and environmental goals.

468) **Ethical banks** including Triodos Bank and the Co-operative bank in the UK, RSF Social Finance in the USA, GLS Bank in Germany, the Alternative Bank in Switzerland, the Banca Etica in Italy, and the Citizens Bank in Canada. These banks invest socially and ethically. The Banca Etica in Italy, for example, is based on the following set of principles: access to finance, in all its forms, is a human right; ethically oriented finance is aware of non-economic consequences of economic actions; efficiency and soberness are components of ethical responsibility; profit produced by the ownership and exchange of money must come from activities oriented towards common well-being and shall have to be equally distributed among all subjects which contribute to its realisation; maximum transparency of all operations is one of the main conditions of all ethical finance activities; the active involvement of shareholders and savers in the company's decision making process must be encouraged; each organisation which accepts and adheres to the principles of ethical finance undertakes to inspire its entire activity to such principles.

469) **Co-operative banks,** including mutual savings banks, building societies, and savings and loan associations. These banks are owned by their members, and governed according to the principle of 'one member one vote'. Co-op banks tend to provide loans to non-members as well as members, and some engage in wholesale markets for money, bonds, and even equity. They are a major part of the banking system in India, and play a significant regional role in Italy and Spain. They usually emphasise their social as well as their financial goals.

470) **Credit Unions** are a form of co-operative bank but are funded primarily by their members' deposits, and do not borrow externally. They are usually formed round a common bond of profession, locality, or religion. They are notably strong in many small developing countries, as well as in Canada, where there are 427 members of the National Federation. They have combined assets of C$117 billion including Vancouver's Vancity (with 410,000 members and assets of C$14 billion) and the Mennonite Credit Union which couples low rates of return on saving with low rates for lending.

471) **Financial guarantee co-operatives,** such as the consorzi fidi (confidi) in Italy, which have been developed to support the financing of co-operatives and other small and medium firms. The members of the consortium elect a committee – usually the most respected entrepreneurs from a range of sectors. These members then study proposals relating to their particular sector (clothing, furniture, engineering, food, etc) and they give their judgement on the quality of the proposal and the prospects of the enterprise. If the judgement is positive, the committee then promises to guarantee a bank loan to the enterprise, backed by a small capital reserve and the personal guarantees of each member of the consortium. This system is very successful, with failure rates of less than 0.5 per cent as against seven per cent for the mainstream financial sector.

472) **Socially motivated disintermediaries** such as Zopa that link together private investors and projects needing capital. In many cases investors are looking for projects that combine social and financial returns.

473) **Bank-based funding for social enterprises** and not-for-profit organisations including Banca Prossima in Italy which is part of the larger banking group Intesa San Paolo.

474) **Business angels** provide finance for social ventures, often with advisory roles, and sometimes supported by networks to link investors and potential projects.

475) **Social wholesale banks,** as opposed to 'retail' banks, could play an important role in diversifying capital markets for social purpose organisations. They would provide a range of finance packages, seeking a blend of social and financial returns (see also method 361).[3]

476) **'eBays' for social investment,** for example, ClearlySo, an online market place for social enterprises and lenders that takes a small margin on the financial transaction.

## Information

Improving market information can help consumers differentiate between organisations and products which cause social and environmental harm and those which do not. This puts pressure on businesses to act in more ethically and environmentally responsible ways.

477) **Labelling and rating systems for social goods** such as food labelling, environmental performance ratings, and publishing information on organisations' carbon footprints.

478) **Social marks and brands to secure a premium for social innovation,** such as 'organic', 'Forest Stewardship' and 'Fairtrade'.

479) **Local kite marks.** For example, a GP's practice in Tiverton, Devon, awards a kite mark to local shops and restaurants that provide healthy food and services.

480) **Consumer guides and reviews.** Since Raymond Postgate founded the 'Good Food Guide' in 1951 and Michael Young founded the Consumer Association and 'Which?' in 1957, consumer guides and commentaries have become commonplace in all sections of publishing, the media, and the internet. They remain critical to the social economy, both in assessing products and services on the basis of social criteria, and in providing publicity to social enterprises. Countries like Cyprus have used the model of a 'Good Food Guide' to upgrade the quality of the island's food and restaurant industry.

481) **Social movement campaigns around corporate conduct** such as the Nestlé baby milk campaign.

## Cards and currencies

Over the past thirty years there has been a widespread growth of store cards and points systems in the commercial sector. Air miles and Nectar points are now part of daily life. They create their own protected economies with discounts for particular products and services from specified places. The growth of parallel mechanisms to favour the social economy has been primarily geared at promoting the local economy. There remains scope for a considerable expansion of these methods to promote social and environmental goods and services.

482) **Local trading currencies.** There are now an estimated 2,500 local currencies operating world wide, particularly payment-voucher systems that are exchangeable for the mainstream currency. In Europe, Germany has more than 20 such currencies. One example is the Chiemgauer which circulates in Prien am Chiemsee in Bavaria. It is sold for an equivalent amount of Euros through local charities who receive a 3 per

The Mayor of Brixton doing his Christmas shopping with Brixton Pounds. The Brixton Pound is the UK's first local currency in an urban area. Image courtesy of Bill Knight/www.knightsight.co.uk

cent commission and accepted as payment in 600 local businesses. In 2008 there were 370,000 Chiemgauer in circulation with an annual turnover of Ch3 million. In the UK, similar initiatives have been recently started by Transition Towns, a group of community-led organisations which focus on energy and climate change issues. The first was the Totnes Pound in Devon and this has been followed by the Lewes Pound in Sussex, the Brixton Pound in London, and the Stroud Pound in Gloucestershire. Like the German currencies, the Brixton Pound is designed to support local businesses and encourage local trade and production. So far, over 70 businesses accept the currency. One Brixton Pound is equivalent to one pound sterling. People can swap their pounds sterling for Brixton pounds at a number of issuing points and then use them in local shops. Local business can then decide to give customers special offers for using the money (see methods on Informal Trading Systems and Currencies, methods 507-510).

## Training and formation

There is growing interest and investment in the development of financial resources for social enterprise. As yet, very few resources have been devoted to labour market development. However, developing skills within the field of social enterprise is critical to the growth and development of the sector.

483) **Specialist academies linked to social economy initiatives,** such as: the University of Mondragón in Spain; the Sekem Academy in Egypt for the research and study of agriculture, pharmaceuticals and medicine from a bio dynamic perspective; and the University of Gastronomic Sciences in Pollenzo and Colorno in Northern Italy, which has grown out of the slow food movement.[4]

484) **Retraining of business leaders to play roles in the social economy,** such as Harvard's Advanced Leadership Programme, pioneered by Rosabeth Moss Kanter and launched in 2008/9.

485) **Leadership training for non-profit organisation managers.** One example is On Purpose, a two-year leadership programme that facilitates, for every participant, four paid placements each of six month's duration, in cutting-edge social businesses and related organisations. Whilst on placement, participants also attend half a day per week of world-class training, delivered by prestigious graduate employers, business schools, think tanks, sector leaders and others.

486) **Lessons in social entrepreneurship** such as the programmes offered by INSEAD and the Skoll Centre for Social Entrepreneurship at Oxford's Saïd Business School. Another model is the School for Social Entrepreneurs (SSE) mentioned in method 206, which provides long-term tailored support to social entrepreneurs to help them hone and develop their entrepreneurial and creative skills. The learning programme is based on 'learning through doing' and peer-learning.

487) **Mutual support networks** such as Community Action Network (CAN) which promotes social entrepreneurship and social enterprise across the UK (see also method 466).

# Markets for social goods

New markets for social goods (or 'bads') can also play a role in accelerating social innovation.

488) **Social markets** such as Slivers-of-Time which link people's spare hours to employer needs. This was originally proposed in the mid-1990s as a Guaranteed Electronic Market (GEM), a web-based market for people to exchange time and loans of products. The model is now implemented in east London.

489) **Markets for 'bads',** such as emissions or waste-disposal trading schemes, and emerging thinking on creating markets for other social 'bads' (such as criminality or unemployment), to accelerate market innovation to meet social and environmental goals.

490) **Markets for 'goods'.** Carbon markets are a means of rewarding carbon reduction, for example the certificates issued for carbon sequestration in soils by the application of compost in Australia. So far there have been no successful pilots of markets for social 'goods', although governments' use of outcome based contracting (for example for getting unemployed people into jobs) comes close.

491) **Social stock exchanges** to measure the performance of social businesses. This would enable investors to trade shares and invest in social-purpose companies and enable those companies to access new forms of finance. Currently a number of social enterprises trade shares through matched bargains between registered buyers and registered sellers on the basis of a price recommended by the Board of Directors. The Rockefeller Foundation has recently announced a study to investigate the viability of a social stock exchange for social enterprises in the UK.

492) **Social indices** such as the FTSE4Good Index Series, which measures the performance of companies that meet globally recognised corporate responsibility standards. This index can be used as a basis for responsible investment, as a way of identifying environmentally and socially responsible companies, and to track their performance over time.

**End notes**

1. For more information on social enterprises and social entrepreneurship see, Nicholls, A. (Ed.) (2006) 'Social Entrepreneurship: new models of sustainable social change.' Oxford: Oxford University Press; Gregory Dees, J. (2001) 'The Meaning of Social Entrepreneurship.' Reformatted and revised, May 30, 2001; Defourny, J. and Nyssens, M. (2008) Social Enterprise in Europe: Recent Trends and Developments. 'Social Enterprise Journal.' Vol. 4, Issue 3, 2008; and Defourny, J. and Nyssens, M. (2008) 'Conceptions of social enterprise in Europe and the United States: convergences and divergences.' Paper presented at the 8th ISTR International Conference and 2nd EMES-ISTR European Conference, Barcelona, July 9-12, 2008; Borzaga, C. and Defourny, J. (Eds) (2001) 'The Emergence of Social Enterprise.' London and New York: Routledge.

2. Emerson, J., Spitzer, J. and Mulhair, G. (2006) 'Blended Value Investing: Capital Opportunities for Social and Environmental Impact.' Geneva: World Economic Forum.

3. For more information see: Office of the Third Sector (2009) ' Social Investment Wholesale Bank: A consultation on the functions and design.' London: Cabinet Office. Available at: http://www.cabinetoffice.gov.uk/media/224319/13528%20social%20bank%20web%20bookmarked.pdf

4. For more information on the Slow Food Movement, see: Petrini, C. (2006) 'Slow Food Revolution.' New York: Rizzoli International.

3

# 4 SUPPORT IN THE INFORMAL OR HOUSEHOLD ECONOMY

Many innovations begin in the informal life of households – a conversation around a coffee, a kitchen table, or a bar. A group of friends or families start living in a new way. Informal associations develop social movements that put pressure on big business or government. Over time what they do may become more formalised and shift into the grant economy and subsequently into the public or market economy. The informal household economy has generally been under-recognised as a source of innovations. But it has played a critical role in fields including the environment and health, usually leading ahead of government and business, and is set to become even more important as issues of ageing and behaviour change become more prominent. In the case of chronic disease, care for young children and the elderly, householders and their networks of support are already the primary source of care.

Within the household economy, we can see a number of emergent trends. One is new forms of mutual action between individuals – whether in the form of open-source software, or web-based social networking around specific issues (there are reportedly 18 million cancer related websites, the great majority generated by those affected by the disease). In these instances the innovations are generated outside the market and outside the state, many of them explicitly so. They have had to develop their own protocols and codes of conduct.

The implications of collaboration of this kind for many contemporary social and economic issues have only begun to be explored, and prompt the question of whether, and how, such systems of highly distributed innovation and mutual support can be encouraged. How do they relate to the state and the

## Housework, paid work and leisure
(Minutes per day and person, latest year available)

**Paid work** ● **Unpaid work** ● **Leisure**

**Note:** Using normalised series for personal care; United States 2005, Finland 1998, France 1999, Germany 2002, Italy 2003, United Kingdom 2001.
**Source:** OECD (2009), *Growing Unequal? Income Distribution and Poverty in OECD Countries*; Paris.

market, and to their terms of funding and employment? Who will provide the necessary tools and platforms? Can they be self-managed, or will they need hosts and intermediaries? These are some of the questions thrown up by this explosive force for innovation.

Many of the organisations providing the platforms and tools that underpin the new systems are developing innovative business models to cover the costs involved – this is especially the case where services are provided for free. Organisations are finding new and alternative ways of raising money – through subscriptions, donations, charging for some services to cover the costs of providing others, selling information on users and so on.[1] In the field of open-source software, they are also creating new terms and conditions for the use of information and products. For users, one of the main challenges now is to navigate through the wide ocean of information available online. There are a range of intermediaries who do this on our behalf, directing us to the most relevant and useful information.

However, this is not just a virtual economy. It is also about care and support in the home and the neighbourhood, volunteering of both time and money, and 'real world' production. There are a whole range of questions about what it takes for households to participate fully in this new world. There is the issue of household time and how it relates to social production and innovation. One of the questions here is how, if at all, it would be possible to acknowledge the voluntary time contributed by the household sector, either individually or collectively, in some form of credits – for cash, public rights or reduced obligations. This is already becoming a key issue in relation to ageing – how to recognise and reward different types of care and volunteering.

There is also the complex issue of managing space – moving beyond the sharp public/private distinction, between the street and the home, to degrees of the social, and how public space is allocated and administered. This question is of course central to current discussions of urban and rural policy (from lighting,

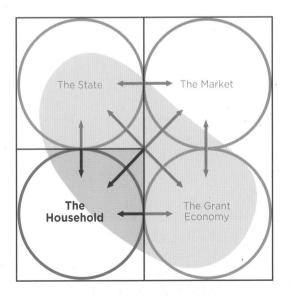

to curfews, to concierges and street wardens, and of course to many aspects of urban transport).

But to spread the benefits of the social economy, we will need to rethink many of the ways in which the household economy relates to the two main sources of finance – the market and the state. Issues such as the distribution of working time, the valorisation of voluntary labour, the content and channels of life skills learning, the role of many of the social and educational services, the arrangements for retirement and unemployment, the size and location of public service centres such as schools and hospitals, and the organisation of public safety – all these will need radical changes.

## Online platforms for collective action

The spread of the internet has made possible a range of new tools to mobilise people and energies quickly and effectively. It has provided an infrastructure to extend the range and capacity of social movements, including consumer movements, as well as enabling new forms of collaborative purchasing and management.

493) **Virtual civil society.** For example, the 'Fever Friend' Network in China, an online community engaged in discussions of controversial and contemporary issues – from mining regulations to urban migration – and the dissemination of contemporary film and culture.

494) **Platforms for aggregating action** at the community level, such as Liftshare, the platform which enables commuters to take part in car-sharing schemes.

495) **Platforms for group purchasing** such as YumShare and food co-ops, and other aggregated purchasing tools where consumers can club together via the internet to achieve savings on their purchases.

496) **Platforms for the gifting of goods** such as Freecycle, whose aim is to keep discarded items out of landfill sites by gifting them. It now has over five million members in 85 countries.

497) **Co-production platforms,** such as Ohmynews in South Korea which provides an online publishing platform for tens of thousands of citizen reporters.

Lee Myung-bak, then Mayor of Seoul, South Korea, shakes hands with Kai Jorgensen, the youngest citizen reporter for OhmyNews, at the OhmyNews citizen forum in Seoul in 2005. OhmyNews is a ground-breaking media-based social innovation that uses web technology to give voice to citizen journalists. Image courtesy of Erik Möller.

498) **Hosts and moderators as online guides.** For example, there is now a Health Information Accreditation Scheme in the UK which gives kite marks to organisations that produce information and moderate websites and forums.

## Propertising not privatising

In the social economy, rather than restricting access to knowledge and information, there is value in diffusing and sharing ideas and information as widely as possible. Online, this means that once the costs of generating information are paid, there is a strong economic case for circulating it for free. Offline, communal or collective forms of innovation can spur innovative and creative uses of assets.

499) **Propertising not privatising.** A distinction can be made between 'propertising' and privatising. Propertising is establishing rights over information and the terms on which it can be used. It introduces the idea of degrees of openness, and of means to strengthen a reciprocal economy by limiting free riders. Examples include open licences.

500) **Open licensing** has redrawn the traditional battle lines between the interests of society and the interests of individual creators – it enables broader access to information while providing incentives to creators by enabling them to retain some rights over their works. Examples include: Creative Commons, Free Documentation, and Open Publication Licences. Essentially, these licences create a freely accessible 'commons' of information with some rights for authors and creators.[2] See Open Knowledge Foundation for more information.

501) **New forms of property ownership** – for example, communities owning their assets, such as the Goodwin Trust in Hull, and Community Land Trusts, both enabling new uses of land and buildings.

502) **Creating a commons of information** to enable broader access. Examples include Open Access Journals which allow academics to publish works online for free.

## Valorising the voluntary

Another set of methods have tried to give formal value to time in the household. This has been achieved through quasi-financial means of payment, encouraging volunteering across sectors, and freeing up people's time to enable them to care for friends and families or volunteer. Many statistical offices are beginning to study time-use in much more detail, opening up new kinds of policy to encourage creative uses of time.

503) **Recognising household time for social production** by valorising voluntary work and support through, for example, public tax credits, community commissioning and grant supported projects.

504) **Policies that create productive time** in the household such as social sabbaticals, or the rights to sabbaticals provided in some professions.

505) **Flexible terms of formal employment** to enable a sustainable informal economy, such as the right to request flexible working time.

506) **Training for volunteers** – the provision of training and incentives for volunteers, and networks for linking volunteers and projects (such as Timebank, Youthnet, etc).

## Informal trading systems and currencies

One way in which household time has been valorised is through 'time bartering' and the development of informal currencies. These currencies are distinct from those issued by regional or municipal governments (like the Patacón in Argentina or the Californian IOUs) or those aimed at encouraging particular types of market purchases (like the Totnes pound). The informal currencies and accounting systems act as a standard of account, a medium of circulation, and a means of payment. They create an economy based on direct household time and can serve as alternatives to mainstream currencies when the latter are unstable or non existent. These generally have an upper limit in terms of size – above which problems of trust and default become a constraint. If they grow too big they also risk encouraging too much attention from tax authorities. Part of our interest here is that these become platforms for innovation in services.

507) **Time banking.** There are some 100 time banks operating in the UK, and another 100 in the pipeline. Many of them operate on a person-to-person model. People 'deposit' time by helping others, and withdraw it when they need something themselves. But recently there have been developments in 'person-to-agency' time banking, such as the model developed by the Wales Institute for Community Currencies and the charity SPICE. SPICE has established more than 40 projects in South Wales whereby institutions like local authorities, schools, colleges and housing associations grant time credits for various kinds of volunteer work – which can then be 'spent' as part payment on buses, meals, internet time, and even social housing rent.

508) **Informal currencies** such as Local Exchange Trading Systems (LETS). LETS involve the creation of notes or equivalents such as Ithaca Hours that represent a specified quantity of labour time. With Ithaca Hours a unit is valued at $10, and while most work is valued as one unit, certain professionals like dentists are allowed to value their hour more highly. Most schemes are limited in size (Ithaca Hours was one of the largest with 1400 members at one time). In the UK where there are some 300 LETS schemes, the average size is 100 members. They are used for person-to-person exchanges and loans, as well as for partial payments in

the market economy.

509) **Social care currencies**. These are also based on time, in this case the time contributed in caring. The largest scheme of this kind is the Japanese Health Care Currency, or 'Fureai Kippu', which evolved when it became apparent that the growing elderly population could not be adequately cared for with government revenue. In this scheme someone works for an hour helping an old person with shopping or housework. If they work outside the hours of 9am to 5pm they get one and a half hours credited to them. If they undertake body care work they get two hours. The time dollars they receive can either be used for themselves or donated to friends and relatives elsewhere. There are some 300 community currencies now operating in Japan, many using smart cards, and focusing on the provision of care.

510) **Informal alternatives to mainstream currencies.** Just as cigarettes became a currency in prisoner of war camps in the Second World War, so mobile airtime has become a currency for mutual and market exchange in Africa. People can send minutes of prepaid airtime to each other by mobile phone using the tool M-Pesa or Me2U, or use prepaid mobile cards for interpersonal transactions or to purchase goods on the market.

## Public spaces for social innovation

The availability of public or communal land increases the household's capacity for innovation by providing the physical space for innovation, and by providing a focal point for initiatives and community action.

511) **Mobilising the street as a unit of innovation** and service delivery through concierges, guardians, and wardens. These kinds of role are important in identifying problems at the hyper-local level and mobilising local residents to innovate solutions.

512) **Reclaiming the streets** and managing public spaces with multiple uses, such as the 'Night for Women' in Bogotá, Colombia, or car-free periods in Canadian cities.

513) **Protests through activity,** such as 'guerrilla gardening', where 'activist' gardeners makeover small plots of public land to cultivate plants and flowers, or 'reverse strikes' such as road building by the unemployed in Sicily.[3]

514) **Extending public spaces for domestic production** such as allotments and opening parts of parks or schools for residents and students to grow flowers, fruits, and vegetables. The Food for Life Partnership (which includes the Focus on Food Campaign, Garden Organic and the Health Education Trust) is a network of schools and communities across the UK which are committed to transforming food culture. As part of the partnership, many schools have set aside some land for growing food and vegetables – which can then be eaten by students at lunchtime.

515) **Community centres** that merge into household activities – childcare, entertainment, meals – and engage citizens in management.

516) **Neighbourhood websites** and other media can become hubs for exchanges and local news. Local residents can find out about initiatives on their block. Examples include hyper-local website Boscalicious

Year 1 pupils from Collaton St Mary Primary School dig up organic potatoes, grown in their school garden. The potatoes were served for lunch that day. Image courtesy of the Food for Life Partnership.

(Boscalicious!) for the residents of Boscombe and W14, for the residents of West Kensington and Fulham in London. EveryBlock in Chicago provides a useful platform for aggregating ultra local data.

## Prosumption

There has been a marked development of users becoming more engaged in the production of services. In the words of Alvin Toffler, they have become 'prosumers' – producers as well as users of services. They are playing a critical role in areas from health and education to recycling and the energy management of the home. Some of this remains at the level of the individual household, but there are a growing number of mutual interest groups and support structures – such as reading groups, asthma networks, homework clubs, or gardening groups – as well as citizens engaging in formal activities through volunteering.

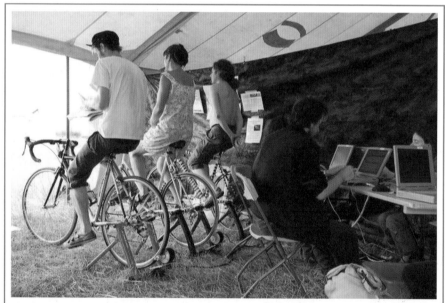

One hour's internet surfing costs 30 minutes pedalling. In 2008, campers converged on Kingsnorth power station for a week of learning, sustainable living and climate action. The event was organised by Camp for Climate Action. Image courtesy of Mike Russell.

517) **Users as producers** – such as the Expert Patients Programme, which teaches users to manage their own health conditions more effectively, and be more confident in their own care. Teachers on the programme are themselves living with long-term conditions. Also, the US-based Citizen Schools organisation, which mobilises citizens who are not teachers to work in schools.

518) **Producer-consumer collaboration,** such as Community Shared Agriculture, in which consumers advance finance to farmers to fund costs for the season, and receive weekly shares of the crop.

## Constructed households as sites of innovation

The long-standing practice of institutionalising those with special needs or who are considered a public danger – in mental hospitals, prisons, care homes, children's homes, or special schools – is being reassessed, and attempts made to retrain people as members of their own or constructed households with a range of external support. In some cases, the institutions themselves have been remodelled as extended families, with the mutual commitments that this entails.

519) **Extending the home.** Residential communities for care and cure, for example San Patrignano, the residential community aimed at cutting drug addiction, based in Italy, that has been replicated in several countries.

520) **Group services for networks of households,** generalising the principle of sheltered accommodation. These are increasingly being developed as a solution for older people – combining individual households, volunteering and shared provision – as with the Elderpower pilot in the US state of Maine. Older people are seen as both users and providers in the system, for example, visiting their peers for friendship, or to remind them to take medication. The pilots claim very significant savings. Safe homes for those with mental illness, such as those provided by Wellink in New Zealand, have a similar model of supported home living.

521) **Co-operative housing as mutual support.** Housing co-operatives such as those run by Niagara Peninsula Homes in Canada require all co-op members to contribute some voluntary time to the maintenance

Lunchtime at San Patrignano. San Patrignano is the largest drug rehabilitation community in the world. It welcomes men and women with drug abuse problems completely free of charge. The community was set up in 1978, when the founder, Vincenzo Muccioli, invited addicts into his home. Since then, San Patrignano has given tens of thousands of men and women a home, a job, training and skills, and the social relationships that are so important in overcoming addiction. Image courtesy of San Patrignano.

of the common areas. They also aim to include accommodation in each of their developments for those with disabilities who might otherwise have to be institutionalised, and to arrange for help and support from neighbours.

## Informal Mutualism

Many new forms of collaboration and co-operation are emerging. These are having profound implications on services and models of collective action.

522) **Developing new models of care and support.** Advising, coaching, mediating, supplementing and communicating for household production.

This could include educational coaching services, relief and back-up for home carers, health coaches, birthing and post birth support, and support teams for end of life care. In many cases, although these supports are not themselves mutual, they provide the underpinning for mutual exchange.

523) **Mutual aid,** on the model of long established organisations like Alcoholics Anonymous and Narcotics Anonymous.

524) **Networks for collaborative production** such as Un Techo para Chile which builds homes for those living in slums. Other examples include free schools and home schooling groups.

525) **User groups** such as rail user groups or park user associations (for example, the Clissold Park User Group) that become champions for new ways of organizing services.

## Social movements

Social movements have been the source of major waves of social innovations over the past 40 years – notably in food, the environment, healthcare, and in transforming the social relations around gender, race, disability, and sexual orientation. They have been largely generated from within the household economy, and have developed innovative forms of distributed network organisation and action, further facilitated by the advent of the internet.

526) **Grass roots campaigns for social change.** The internet has accelerated the spread of grass roots-led social campaigns – especially those focused on lifestyle innovation and transformation. Examples include the green movement (for example, Transition Towns) but also Slow Food, a network of over 100,000 people in 132 countries who campaign against 'fast food and fast life' in favour of ethically sourced and locally produced quality food.

527) **Our Space.** Web based platforms for organising grass roots campaigns. In the last year alone, Facebook has been used to mobilise protesters against knife crime, the military Junta in Burma, and FARC. Oscar Morales, founder of the Facebook group One Million Voices against FARC (which now has over 400,000 members) used the social networking site to organise a massive protest against the rebel forces in February 2008. Over a million people marched through the streets of Bogotá

carrying banners with the slogan – 'no more kidnappings, no more deaths, no more FARC'. Simultaneous protests were held in 200 other cities including London, Los Angeles, Cairo, Sydney, Tokyo, Miami, Paris, Tel-Aviv, and Rome. According to Morales, 'the February 4th protest was a big slap in the face to FARC, who saw that its ideals were no longer supported by the people, and many members of FARC then started abandoning the group….digital platforms are a means to social liberties…we proved that the digitally connected few can connect the masses.'[4]

**End notes**

1. See Murray, R., Caulier-Grice, J. and Mulgan, G. (2009) 'Social Venturing.' London: NESTA.
2. www.okfn.org
3. Dolci, D. (1960) 'Outlaws of Partinico.' London: McGibbon and Kee.
4. Morales, O. (2008) The Alliance of Youth Movements Summit, 4 December, Columbia School of Law, New York. For more information on the summit, see: http://info.howcast.com/youthmovements/summit/agenda

# BIBLIOGRAPHY

Andrea Cornwall and Vera Schattan Coelho (eds), Spaces for Change, Zed Books, 2007.

Augusto Boal, Theatre of the Oppressed, Pluto Press, 1979, Augusto Boal, Games for Actors and Non-actors, Routledge, 2002 and Legislative Theatre: Using Performance to Make Politics, Routledge, 1998.

Carlo Petrini, Slow Food Revolution, Rizzoli International, 2006.

Christopher Alexander et al, A Pattern Language: Towns, Buildings, Construction, New York, Oxford University Press, 1977, and, The Nature of Order, Volume 2, The Centre for Environmental Structure, 2002.

Colin Burns, Hilary Cottam, Chris Vanstone and Jennie Winhall, Transformation Design, RED PAPER 02, London, Design Council, 2006.

Danilo Dolci, Outlaws of Partinico, McGibbon and Key, 1957.

Edgar Morin, On Complexity, Cresskill, NJ, Hampton Press, 2007.

Edward W Deming, Out of the Crisis: quality, productivity and competitive position, Cambridge, MIT Press, 1986.

Eric Beinhocker, The Origin of Wealth, Random House, 2007.

Fernando Flores, Charles Spinosa and Hubert Dreyfus, Disclosing New Worlds: Entrepreneurship, Democratic Action, and the Cultivation of Solidarity, Cambridge, MIT Press, 1999.

Geoff Andrews, The Slow Food Story, Pluto Press, 2008.

Hilary Wainwright, Public Service Reform But Not As We Know It, Picnic, 2009.

Ibrahim Abouleish, Sekem: A sustainable community in the Egyptian Desert, Floris Books, 2005.

Jaime Lerner, Acupuntura Urbana, Rio de Janeiro, Editora Record, 2003.

Jim Maxmin and Soshana Zuboff, The Support Economy: Why Corporations are Failing Individuals and the Next Episode of Capitalism, Penguin, 2004.

John Dewey, Experience and Education, New York, Collier Books, 1938.

John Thackara, Designing in a Complex World, Cambridge, MIT Press, 2005.

Leonardo Avritzer, Participatory Institutions in Democratic Brazil, Woodrow Wilson Centre Press, 2009.

Ludwig Fleck, Genesis and Development of a Scientific Fact, Chicago, University of Chicago Press, 1979.

M.P. Parameswaran, Democracy by the People, Alternatives Asia, 2008.

Mahatma Gandhi, Hind Swaraj, Cambridge, 1997.

Mark H. Moore, Creating Public Value: Strategic Management in Government, Cambridge, Harvard University Press, 1995.

Muhammad Yunus, Banker to the Poor, Aurum Press, 2003.

Nicholas Albery and Nick Temple, World's Greatest Ideas: An Encyclopaedia Of Social Inventions (and a related series of books of social inventions published during the 1990s), New Society Publishers, 2001.

Pooran Desai, One Planet Communities, John Wiley, 2010.

Robert Chambers, Participatory Workshops: a sourcebook of 21 sets of ideas and activities, London, Earthscan, 2002 and Revolutions in Development Inquiry, Earthscan, 2008.

Roberto Mangabeira Unger, The Self Awakened: Pragmatism Unbound, Cambridge, Harvard University Press, 2009.

Stephen Goldsmith et al, The Power of Social Innovation: How Civic Entrepreneurs Ignite Community Networks for Good, Jossey Bass, 2010.

William McDonough and Michael Braungart, Cradle to Cradle, North Point Press, 2002.

Walter Stahel, The Performance Economy, Palgrave Macmillan, 2006.

# INDEX

# ACKNOWLEDGEMENTS

We would like to acknowledge the help and support from colleagues at NESTA – in particular Michael Harris and Laura Bunt for their encouragement, patience and perceptive comments on the text.

We would also like to thank colleagues at the Young Foundation, especially Will Norman for his editorial comments, and Louise Pulford, Ginny Lee, Cynthia Shanmugalingam, Jack Graham, Lauren Kahn, Sarah Hewes, Alex Watson, Jessica Daggers, David Jenkins and Isobel Colchester for their contributions.

Finally, we are indebted to all those who contributed ideas, photographs, and methods. This support has been invaluable, and we are hugely grateful.

Thanks also to the many people who have contributed both directly and indirectly to this project including Peter Ramsden, David Barrie, Bethany Murray, Hamish McCardle, Bill Knight, Hilary Cottam at Participle, Eric Cadora at the Justice Mapping Center, SILK, MindLab, The Centre for Social Innovation, Kennisland, Social Innovation Camp, The Design Council, The Hope Institute, Plane Stupid, AmericaSpeaks, Dialogue Café, Helsinki Design Lab, Google Inc, Un Techo para Chile, Riversimple, Working Rite, Danone Communities, Sekem, Social Innovation Exchange, My Football Club, Pratham, Green Homes, In Control, Everdale, The Climate Project, Australian Social Innovation Exchange, School for Social Entrepreneurs, Ten UK, Camp for Climate Action, Transition Towns, the Innovation Unit, Innovation Exchange, the Hub, MaRS Discovery District, Fuping Development Centre, 27e Region, The Ash Institute for Democratic Governance and Innovation at Harvard University's John F. Kennedy School of Government, The Prosperity Initiative, Vodafone, The Brixton Pound, SPICE, The Food for Life Partnership, San Patrignano and many others.

This publication represents solely the views of the authors and does not necessarily represent the views of NESTA or the Young Foundation. Any errors or omissions are those of the authors.